North Afri
Cooking

North African Cooking

EXOTIC DELIGHTS FROM MOROCCO, TUNISIA, ALGERIA AND EGYPT

Hilaire Walden

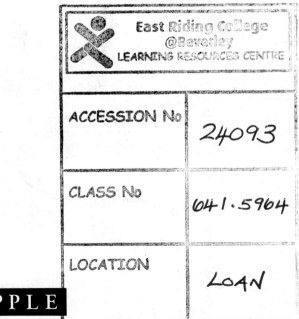
APPLE

A QUINTET BOOK

This edition published in 2000 by
Apple Press
6 Blundell Street
London N7 9BH

ISBN 1-84092-261-3

This book was designed and produced by
Quintet Publishing Limited
6 Blundell Street
London N7 9BH

Creative Director: Richard Dewing
Designer: Ian Hunt
Project Editor: Claire Tennant-Scull
Editor: Lesley Ellis
Photographer: David Armstrong

Typeset in Great Britain by
Central Southern Typesetters, Eastbourne
Manufactured in Hong Kong by
Regent Publishing Services Limited
Printed in Hong Kong by
Midas Printing Limited

ACKNOWLEDGEMENTS
Quintet Publishing would like to thank The Kasbah,
London, for providing North African ceramics and
metalware; also Evergreen and Gorgeous, London N16,
for providing flowers for photography

Location photography by Nick Bailey and Life File

Contents

Introduction

Bordering the southern Mediterranean Sea are the three countries of Algeria, Morocco and Tunisia, which were once known as the Maghreb and today make up the region of North Africa.

The cuisine of this region is now popular throughout the world – evocative, colourful and sophisticated, it is full of the romance of North Africa, and rich with the flavours of warm spices.

Together the three countries of North Africa offer a very distinctive style of cookery, with many similarities and shared themes that cross the region: slow-simmered, spicy casseroles called *tagines,* for example, are found throughout the area, as are steamed dishes of *couscous* grains, aromatic lamb recipes, colourful and astonishingly sweet desserts and sweetmeats, and pies and pastries made from a special wafer-thin pastry called *warka.*

Each country has its own unique characteristics, of course; its own favourite spices and national dishes: Moroccans like full, rich flavours, and often include saffron in their cooking; Tunisians have a penchant for more highly flavoured, fiery dishes; while Algerians prefer their dishes rather less spicy.

North African cuisine has its roots in many different places and ancient cultures. The succession of different peoples who have invaded, traded with or visited North Africa over the centuries have all left their legacies: the Persians contributed a predilection for combining meat and fruit; the famous pigeon pie called *b'stilla* was brought from Andalusia via the Moors; and Tunisian *chakchouka,* a dish of pepper, tomato and egg, has its origins in Turkish *menemen.*

Two thousand years ago the countries of Morocco, Tunisia, Algeria and Libya were just one country, known as the Maghreb. It was the home of Christians, the pale-skinned, fair-haired and fine-featured nomadic Berbers. The diet and traditions of the Berbers and the nomadic Bedouin Arabs is still evident today in the use of dates, *smen* (a cooked and aged butter) and grains. Ingenuity stemmed from necessity and centuries ago the Bedouin people discovered the versatility of different grains. They discovered how to use fermented grains as a natural "starter" to produce leavened breads, and some sources claim that they developed dried pasta as a way of preserving dough during their long treks

RIGHT *Imposing North African landscape silhouetted by cloudless, intense blue skies*

RIGHT *Tinmel Mihrab, Morocco*

across the desert, and then took it with them when they landed in Sicily, from where it spread to the rest of Italy.

North Africa has a long coastline so there has always been easy access for traders and invaders. In the first century BC, Phoenician traders arrived and introduced dried sausages, forerunners of the spicy little Algerian sausages called *merguez,* which had been devised as a way of preserving meat during the traders' lengthy journeyings. Next came the Carthaginians who were responsible for introducing durum wheat and its byproduct, semolina. This was adapted by the Berbers into *couscous,* which is today a staple of the area.

With the invading Arabs of the seventh century came the Muslim religion which since then has become the strongest cultural influence in the region, dictating food as well as every other aspect of life. The Arabs, who had long been the spice merchants of the world, also brought many exotic spices such as saffron, nutmeg, ginger, cloves and cinnamon from the Spice Islands.

Moors returning voluntarily, or expelled, from Spain brought back the foods of Andalusia such as olives and olive oil. Fruits such as oranges, plums and peaches also crossed the Mediterranean.

In the 14th century it was the turn of Turkish Ottomans, who brought them sweet and delicate pastries. Later, European traders and colonizers arrived and relics of their influence include tea from British merchants, who disposed of large quantities in Tangiers and Mogador when they were seeking new markets during the Crimean War.

Today, restaurant menus may be written in Spanish, English or French. French sophistication has been absorbed into the essence of the Maghreb. French is spoken in all three countries, particularly Algeria, which was occupied longest by the French. Middle-class Algerians speak French in preference to Arabic and housewives buy French-style baguettes rather than Arabic *kesra.*

Some ingredients, now so characteristic of North African cooking, were originally imported from the New World: tomatoes, potatoes, courgettes, and chillies and peppers which also yield the paprika and cayenne pepper so important to the local cooking.

Eating in North Africa

Hospitality is important to the people of North Africa and meals are prepared as abundant offerings to family, friends, and even casual passers-by who drop by or are invited to come in; and many varied dishes are set on the table. Ancient rituals of eating have been kept alive by nomadic tribes. Feasts at which *mechoui* (spit-roast whole lamb) is the main dish are still enjoyed by the Bedouins. *Mechoui* has been adapted in cities, and the lamb is halved or quartered before being roasted over a brazier.

In middle-class North African homes meals are served with formal elegance. Bright mosaics decorate the walls of the dining room and there are richly woven carpets, Baroque silverware and hand-carved furniture. Diners sit at low tables (*tbla* or *mida*) and, in silence, a servant or young member of the family will take a bowl of perfumed water around the diners in turn, holding it beneath their hands and pouring water over them from an *ied ettas*; a towel is then proffered.

Food is traditionally eaten with the thumb, forefinger and middle finger of the right hand (the left hand is considered unclean); to eat with one finger is considered a sign of hatred, to eat with two shows pride, three accords with the Prophet Mohammed, while to eat with four or five fingers is a sign of gluttony.

Bread is used to help mop up the cooking juices and sauces, and to carry the food to the mouth. Wheat in the form of couscous and bread, not rice, is the main staple of the diet.

In a land where literacy levels have been very low, cooking knowledge and recipes have been handed down by word of mouth from mother to daughter. Cooking has always been considered women's work and a North African wife spends much of her time preparing food. On occasions of family feasts, female relatives and friends all gather in the kitchen to help with the preparations, and so share and pass on their recipes, experience and knowledge.

Cooking Equipment

North African kitchens are very simple with the minimum of equipment; labour is cheap and plentiful so tasks are done by hand, not with gadgets. Ovens are rare, even in restaurant kitchens. Food to be baked is taken to the neighbourhood communal oven. There is also a lack of weighing equipment; measuring is done by eye and feel.

There are no chairs in a traditional kitchen, and often even a table is absent; cooks squat when both mixing and cooking on the brazier. There may be just a stool or two perhaps, or even an old carpet folded to act as a seat for the cook. In the average traditional country kitchen the most usual equipment to be found is:

COUSCOUSIER consists of two parts, a tin, aluminium, stainless steel or earthenware bottom part (*gdra*) in which to cook meat, poultry and vegetables, and a *kskas,* the top part. This holds the *couscous* and has a perforated base and sits snugly on the *gdra* so the steam from below permeates and flavours the grain. A saucepan with a tightly fitting colander, or a steamer can be used instead.

GENBURA a glazed earthenware pot, which is very broad in relation to its height; used for storing water.

GHORBAL a sieve with a perforated leather bottom for gauging the coarseness of semolina.

GSAA a large, flat wooden or unglazed earthenware dish with a 10 cm/4 in sloping lip which is used for mixing dough for cakes, breads and pastries, and to mix and aerate semolina grains for *couscous*.

KHABIAS fairly high but not very wide earthenware jars, glazed on the inside, for preserving meat and storing flour, corn and pulses.

MGHORFA a large wooden spoon.

M'IDOURNA OR T'BECK a round, flat basket which can also be used for aerating semolina grains for *couscous*.

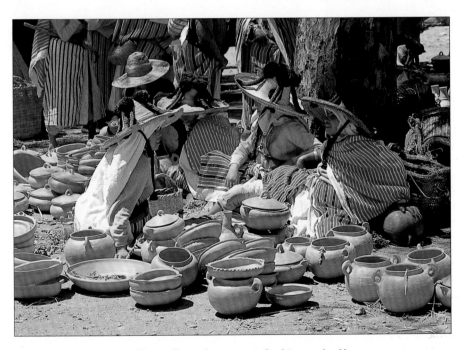

ABOVE *Women selling earthenware pots in Oued-Laou market, Morocco*

ABOVE *Brassware at Marrakech market, Morocco*

MEHRAZ a heavy brass mortar and pestle for pounding spices and herbs (wood is not used as it would soon become tainted).

QA TAGINE a deep copper dish in which a *tagine slaoui* is placed when it is served, to protect the table.

TAGINE SLAOUI also often known simply as a *tagine,* this is a round earthenware pot with a glazed lid shaped like a coolie's hat, which is used to cook stews of meat, fish, poultry or vegetables. In North Africa, *tagines* are cooked over charcoal but if using a traditional earthenware *tagine* over the direct heat of a gas or electric hob it is best to use a heat diffusing mat to protect it (but check with the handbook for electric cookers).

There will also probably be a few copper *taouas* (casseroles) in most kitchens, a pan for frying fish or almonds, knives and earthenware bottles for keeping spices.

For cooking on there is a small round charcoal brazier, usually round and of unglazed earthenware, called a *kanoun* or *mjmar,* specially designed to hold the round bottom of a *tagine* safely in place with its three raised points. The low, even heat that can be achieved with a charcoal fire is ideal for the slow-cooking *tagines* need if they are to be at their most succulent and flavoursome. This type of heat is also ideal for allowing richly flavoured sauces to simmer very gently, but charcoal can also be adjusted to give a fiercer heat for cooking kebabs, brochettes and fish.

Other traditional equipment includes a large basket with a decorated pointed lid called a *t'bicka,* which is used for serving bread; a *t'bsil dial warka,* which is a large round flat tin-covered dish with a shallow rim that is used, bottom-side up, for baking *warka* and bottom-side down, to bake *b'stilla.*

Flavours of North Africa

CHERMOULA a distinctive mixture of onion, coriander, garlic, chillies and spices widely used to bring character and flavour to many dishes. *Chermoula* is used as a marinade for grilled, baked or braised fish, poultry, lamb and game such as rabbit. The combination and proportions of ingredients vary from cook to cook, and also according to the kind of food to be marinated and the character of dish required.

See page 126 for basic *Chermoula* recipes that can be used in other recipes.

COUSCOUS is made from semolina that has been ground, moistened and rolled in flour. Most *couscous* now on sale is pre-cooked and needs only to be moistened and steamed to heat through and separate the grains. Butter is usually rubbed into *couscous* to help separate and enrich the grains. To prepare *couscous* for four people, put 450 g/1 lb pre-cooked *couscous* in a bowl, pour over about 300 ml/½ pint boiling water, stir well and leave for ten minutes. Add another 300 ml/½ pint water and two teaspoons olive oil and fork through the *couscous* to make sure the grains separate, then leave for ten minutes until swollen and tender but still separate. Put into a steamer and place, uncovered, over a saucepan of boiling water for ten minutes, or for about 20 minutes over a pot of gently cooking meat and vegetables. Fork through the *couscous* to separate the grains then turn onto a warm large serving plate. Dot with butter, add seasoning and stir. Form into a mound with a large well in the centre into which to put the meat and vegetables.

HERBS these are limited to flat-leaved, Continental parsley and coriander, which are regularly used fresh by the bunchful, and mint which is used less abundantly and usually dried.

OLIVE OIL many North African cooks use large amounts of oil – too much for most Western tastes. The oil not only adds flavour but binds together the ingredients and thickens dishes such as *tagines*. For the recipes in this book, the amounts of oil have been reduced to suit Western palates.

RAS EL HANOUT literally means "head of the shop" or "shopkeeper's choice". It is a warming old, complicated mixture of many powdered spices, roots, barks and flowers. Sometimes there are as few as ten, often as many as 20 or 25, perhaps even more different ingredients. Ingredients and proportions vary from cook to cook, but *ras el hanout* is generally thought to contain such aphrodisiacs as cantharides (Spanish fly). A simplified recipe for a home-made version of *Ras el Hanout* is on page 118.

SMEN is a type of preserved clarified butter prepared in a way similar to Indian *ghee*; it may be flavoured with wild herbs. It has quite a potent cheesey taste that takes a little getting used to, especially for eating on bread. In cooking, *smen* lends a characteristic flavour to *tagines*, *k'dras* and *couscous*. In some Fez and Berber households, *smen* is packed in glass jars and kept for years, gradually becoming darker and more pungent with time.

See page 120 for a home-made version of *smen*.

SPICES spices are the backbone of North African cooking. They are used with generosity but judiciousness and great skill add character to cooking and enhance the taste of other ingredients. Spices also stimulate the appetite by producing enticing aromas and colour to food, and aid digestion.

The most popular, indeed essential, spices are cumin, paprika, saffron, ginger, cinnamon, coriander and cayenne. Because of the frequency with which the spices are used in North African kitchens they never have time to go stale and it is important when you are cooking these recipes to ensure that the spices you use are absolutely fresh.

WARKA this is a tissue-thin pastry. It is made by patting small balls of dough 18 or 20 times in succession in a series of concentric circles, overlapping the circles slightly, on a metal domed metal surface heated over a brazier. In this way a wide, circular sheet of extremely thin, lacy, delicate pastry is made. It takes practice, skill and patience to make and nowadays is often bought ready-made from specialist shops. Filo pastry is the best alternative for Western cooks or, in some recipes, Chinese spring roll wrappers.

Wines of the Region

Many North Africans will not drink wine as they are governed by the rules of Islam, which forbid the consumption of alcohol. However, wine production, and consumption, pre-dates the arrival of Islam. The Romans introduced the vine to the area. It thrived in the favourable climate and soil conditions, and winemaking spread rapidly until the fall of the Roman Empire. Winemaking remained in decline until the French and Spanish began colonization and planted southern French and, to a lesser extent, Spanish grape varieties. When Morocco gained independence in 1956 the government instituted a quality control system based on the French Appellation Controlle system. Tunisia and Algeria soon followed suit. The area under vines again rapidly increased and in 1973 the wine industry was officially classified as a national industry in Morocco. But since then Islam has exercised its influence again and viticulture has declined. The vast majority of North African wines are bulk varieties, mainly red, for blending but some pleasant ones for local drinking can be found.

Variations on a Theme

Inevitably, when covering the cuisine of three similar, neighbouring countries quite a number of dishes will cross national boundaries. However, each country puts its own stamp on a recipe, using slightly different methods and flavourings. Various versions of the same dish may also be met in different regions, towns, villages, and even in different homes. Don't be surprised, therefore, if you come across a dish with the same name but which tastes different from the one I have given. You may also come across different spellings for the same recipe – names and spellings are a minefield in North Africa. Each country, and sometimes individual districts within a country, have their own version of Arabic. Furthermore, phonetic French or English spellings of North African dishes can present a problem. Moroccan Arabic, in contrast to classical Arabic, is a spoken language and therefore phonetic spellings vary enormously. For example, *b'stilla,* can also be spelt *bisteeya, bstila, pstilla,* and *pasteeya,* and the ultra-thin pastry used to make it can be spelt *warka* or *ouarka.*

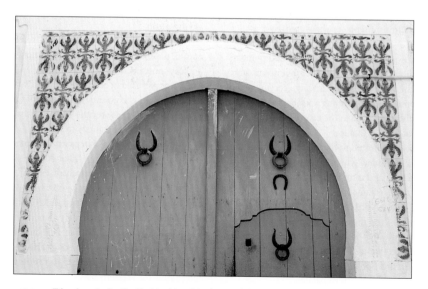

ABOVE *Tiles above the familiar Tunisian blue of the door symbolising God's presence. Sidi Bon Said, Tunisia*

1

Soups

North African soups are spicy, substantial and nourishing, and are generally served as a supper dish. The most famous soup of all is the Moslem *Harira,* traditionally eaten at sundown during the month of Ramadan to break the day's fast, although it is eaten at other times of the year too.

Chunky Tunisian Fish Soup

——— BROUDOU BIL HOUT ———

*There are clear similarities between this substantial fish soup and bouillabaisse,
which comes from the other side of the Mediterranean. Any selection of fish and
shellfish can be used except oily fish such as mackerel and sardines. If you like,
you can use the heads, tails, skin and bones to make fish stock for the soup.*

SERVES 6-8

3 tbsp olive oil
2 onions, chopped
3 garlic cloves, chopped
1 red pepper, chopped
about 1 tsp Harissa (see
  page 120)
1/4 tsp crushed saffron
  threads
1/4–1/2 tsp ground
  cinnamon
1/4–1/2 tsp ground cumin
1 fennel bulb, diced,
  feathery fronds reserved

2 large potatoes, chopped
2 1/2–3 tbsp lemon juice
1.5 ltr/2 1/2 pt fish stock or
  water
2 kg/4 1/2 lb mixed fish and
  shellfish, prepared
4 well-flavoured tomatoes,
  peeled, seeded and
  chopped
1 large bunch of mixed
  coriander and parsley,
  finely chopped
salt and pepper
good bread, to serve

Heat the oil in a large saucepan, then fry the onion
until softened but not coloured. Add the garlic and
red pepper, cook for 2–3 minutes then stir in the
Harissa, spices, fennel, potatoes, lemon juice and
stock or water. Bring to the boil then simmer for
about 20 minutes until the potatoes are almost
cooked. Add the fish, tomatoes, herbs, seasoning
and water as necessary, and cook gently until the
fish is tender. Serve sprinkled with the reserved
fennel fronds and accompanied by good bread.

ABOVE *Fisher boats at Medique, Morocco*

Lentil Soup

*For centuries lentils have provided a simple, adaptable, accessible and portable
source of protein and calories; Arab cooks have been using them since the time of
the ancient Sumerians and Egyptians.*

SERVES 6–8

2 tbsp olive oil

1 Spanish onion, finely
  chopped

2 garlic cloves, chopped

350 g/12 oz shin of veal,
  chopped

1/2 tsp each ground cumin
  and cinnamon

1/4 tsp cayenne pepper

175 g/6 oz green lentils

1.5 ltr/2 1/2 pt water

3 small-to-medium carrots,
  diced

3 celery sticks, chopped

2 potatoes, diced

salt and pepper

1 bunch of coriander,
  coarsely chopped

lemon juice

Boil the lentils in a pan of water for at least 10
minutes, drain, and set aside. Heat the oil in a pan,
then cook the onion, garlic and veal, stirring
frequently, until the onion is soft. Stir in the spices
until fragrant, then add the lentils and water. Bring
to the boil and skin the scum from the surface. Partly
cover and simmer for about one hour until the meat
is tender.

Add the vegetables and cook for a further 30–40
minutes. Season and stir in the coriander, and lemon
juice to taste. Serve straight away.

Chickpea Soup

——— LABLABI ———

*Lablabi is a thick garlicky soup from Tunisia. It is usually extremely rich, but I
have reduced the amount of oil here. The taste of all the garlic mellows with the
long cooking. Add some ground spices, such as cumin, coriander and paprika if
you like.*

SERVES 4

6 tbsp olive oil

10 garlic cloves, crushed

350 g/12 oz chickpeas,
  soaked overnight and
  drained

1.8 ltr/4 pt water

1 Spanish onion, finely
  chopped

2 carrots, chopped

1 head of celery, chopped

salt and pepper

lemon juice

1 bunch of coriander,
  chopped

Heat 4 tbsps oil in a large pan, then cook the garlic
until fragrant. Stir in the chickpeas then add the
water and bring to the boil. Skim the scum from the
surface, then simmer until the chickpeas are tender.

Meanwhile, heat the remaining oil in a flameproof
earthenware casserole, add the onion, carrots and
celery, cover and cook gently for about 20 minutes.

Add the vegetables to the beans, then purée half
the mixture in a food processor or blender, or rub
through a sieve. Stir back into the soup and reheat.
Add seasoning and lemon juice to taste and sprinkle
with coriander.

LEFT *Lentil Soup*

Lamb and Vegetable Soup with Vermicelli

———— CHORBAH ————

Variations of this thickened vermicelli soup are found throughout the Maghreb, although the name may vary slightly. Traditionally, lamb in the Maghreb is tough so the meat would be simmered in one piece, with the bones, for about one hour first, to make sure it was sufficiently tender to eat. As our modern-day lamb is more tender to start with, the cooking time has been reduced.

SERVES 6

4 onions, chopped
3 garlic cloves, chopped
3 red peppers, chopped
675 g/1½ lb lean lamb, cubed
3 tbsp olive oil
2 lamb bones, cracked
1.75 ltr/3¼ pt stock or water

salt and pepper
pinch of crushed dried red chillies
4 tomatoes, chopped
115 g/4 oz dried apricots
1–1½ tbsp chopped mint leaves
115 g/4 oz vermicelli
1 tbsp lemon juice
chopped fresh parsley and mint, to garnish

Heat the oil in a large saucepan, then cook the onions, garlic, peppers and lamb, stirring occasionally, for about 10 minutes. Add the bones, stock, seasoning, chilli, tomatoes, apricots and mint and bring just to the boil then simmer for about 1¼–1½ hours until the lamb is very tender.

Bring to the boil, add the vermicelli and cook for 5 minutes until tender. Pour the soup into a warmed tureen, stir in the lemon juice and garnish with chopped parsley and mint.

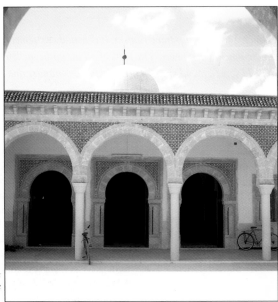

RIGHT *North Africa shows the Middle Eastern influence in its architecture*

Harira

*At sunset in Morocco during the month of Ramadan, a firing cannon signals the
end of the day's fast, and heralds the time to sit down to rich, red and spicy
Harira. Harira is not eaten only at Ramadan, however.
Chicken can be used instead of lamb and using chicken stock in place of water,
to make a lighter soup, or meat may be omitted altogether and another vegetable
or two, such as aubergines and courgettes, added to make a vegetarian soup.
The soup is sometimes thickened at the end of cooking with flour, or with eggs.*

SERVES 6

2 tbsp olive oil
*225 g/8 oz lean lamb,
  cubed*
1 onion, chopped
*115 g/4 oz chickpeas,
  soaked overnight and
  drained*
1.5 ltr/2½ pt water
115 g/4 oz red lentils
salt and pepper

*400 g/14 oz tomatoes,
  peeled, seeded and
  chopped*
1 tbsp tomato purée
1 tsp ground cinnamon
*1 red pepper, seeded and
  chopped*
50 g/2 oz vermicelli
*1 bunch of coriander,
  chopped*
lemon wedges, to serve

Heat the oil in a large saucepan, then fry the lamb until lightly and evenly browned. Stir in the onion and cook gently until softened. Add the chickpeas and water, bring to the boil, then cover and simmer for 1 hour, or until the chickpeas are almost tender.

Add the lentils, tomatoes, tomato purée, cinnamon and red pepper and simmer for about 15 minutes. Then add the vermicelli, bring to the boil and simmer for a further 15 minutes, until the lentils and vermicelli are tender. Stir in the coriander and seasoning. Serve with lemon wedges.

ABOVE *Light and shade contrast vividly in the Algerian desert*

Fish, Tomato and Potato Soup

———— SHORBA BIL HOUT ————

Any white fish could be used for this Algerian soup, but I find that delicate or indeterminately flavoured fish, such as plaice, sole and whiting, are overpowered by the other ingredients, but cod or haddock would be suitable. Although not traditional, I sometimes also include trout.

SERVES 6

3 tbsp olive oil
2 onions, chopped
4 garlic cloves, crushed
450 g/1 lb well-flavoured
    tomatoes, peeled, seeded
    and chopped
1¹/₂ tsp paprika pepper
pinch of cayenne pepper
good pinch of crushed
    saffron threads

2 bay leaves
1–1¹/₂ tsp fresh thyme
2 large potatoes, cubed
2.4 ltr/4 pt water
1 kg/2¹/₄ lb firm white fish
    fillets, skinned
2¹/₂–4 tbsp lemon juice
salt and pepper
2 eggs

Heat the oil in a large saucepan, then fry the onion until softened but not coloured. Add the garlic and tomatoes and cook for about 10 minutes until the tomatoes have given up some of their liquid. Thoroughly stir in the paprika, cayenne, saffron, herbs and potatoes then add the water and bring to the boil. Simmer for about 15 minutes until the potatoes are almost cooked. Then, add the fish and cook very gently until it flakes.

Discard the bay leaves and purée the soup in a blender or by rubbing through a sieve. Return to the pan and reheat, adding extra water if it is too thick – it will thicken slightly more when the eggs are added. Add lemon juice and seasoning to taste.

In a small bowl, beat the eggs with a ladleful of the soup. Over a low heat, stir the egg mix into the soup and heat gently, stirring, until thickened; do not allow to boil.

2

Starters, Salads and Snacks

Quite a number of North African so-called salads are not salads as we know them, but dips or purées. Others are made of a type of vegetable or combination of vegetables, and may be cooked or raw. You can serve a selection of salads as a first course, and then leave them on the table throughout the meal. They can also be served as snacks if accompanied by good bread.

Grilled Red Pepper and Tomato Salad

SALADE DE POIVRONS ET TOMATOES

Grilling the red peppers and tomatoes (which is traditionally done over a barbecue) gives them a delicious smoky taste and silky texture. This salad comes from Morocco and can be flavoured with cumin and cayenne if you like, and thin strips or dice half of a preserved lemon. It can be served as a first course, or with grilled meats, poultry or fish.

SERVES 4

3 large red or green
  peppers
4 well-flavoured tomatoes
2 garlic cloves, finely
  chopped

salt and pepper
1 small bunch of parsley,
  chopped, if liked

Preheat the grill and place the peppers and tomatoes in a grill pan then grill them, turning occasionally until evenly charred and blistered. Leave until cool enough to handle, then remove and discard the skins. Remove and discard the cores and seeds. Dice the flesh, place in a bowl, and mix together.

Sprinkle over the garlic, seasoning and parsley, cover and chill. Drain off any excess liquid before serving.

Grilled Red Pepper Salad with Eggs

SALATAT MESHWIYA

The capers and lemon juice give a bright piquancy to this brilliantly coloured salad.

SERVES 4

4 red peppers, halved
2 tbsp lemon juice
4 tbsp olive oil
salt and pepper
4 well-flavoured tomatoes,
  sliced

1 red onion, sliced
3 hard-boiled eggs
2 tsp capers
oil-cured black olives and
  chopped fresh parsley for
  garnish

Preheat the grill, place the peppers in a grill pan and cook, turning occasionally until charred and blistered. Leave until cool enough to handle then, holding each pepper-half in turn over a bowl to catch the juices, remove and discard the skin. Slice the peppers.

Add the lemon juice, oil and seasoning to the bowl and whisk together with the pepper juices.

Mix the peppers with the tomatoes, onion, eggs and capers, pour over the dressing and sprinkle with olives and chopped parsley.

RIGHT *Grilled Red Pepper and Tomato Salad*

Bulgar, Red Pepper, Cucumber and Cheese Salad

Oil-cured black olives can also be added to this salad just before serving,
if you like.

SERVES 4–6

225 g/8 oz bulgar wheat
300 ml/½ pt boiling water
4 tbsp olive oil
3 tbsp lemon juice
2 tbsp chopped fresh mint
3 tbsp chopped fresh
   coriander
salt and pepper

1 red pepper, grilled,
   peeled and sliced
1 bunch of plump spring
   onions, chopped
2 garlic cloves, chopped
½ cucumber, coarsely
   chopped
115 g/4 oz feta cheese,
   crumbled
lime wedges, to serve

Place the bulgar wheat in a large bowl, add the boiling water and leave to soak for 30 minutes, stirring occasionally with a fork, until the water has been absorbed.

In a mixing bowl, whisk together the oil, lemon juice and seasoning. Pour oil mixture over the bulgar wheat, add the herbs and mix well. Then mix in the remaining ingredients. Cover and chill until required. Serve garnished with lime wedges.

Spiced Whole Carrot Salad

SERVES 4

450 g/1 lb small carrots
1 garlic clove
½ tsp paprika
½ tsp ground cumin
pinch each of ground
   cinnamon, cayenne and
   sugar

3 tbsp lemon juice
2 tbsp fresh chopped
   parsley
1½ tbsp olive oil
salt

Cook the carrots and garlic in a pan of boiling salted water until just tender. Drain. Discard the garlic and slice the carrots. Place in a serving dish.

In a small bowl, mix together the spices, sugar and lemon juice, then pour over the carrots and toss together. Cover and chill.

Just before serving, sprinkle over the parsley and olive oil.

LEFT *Bulgar, Red Pepper,*
Cucumber and Cheese Salad

Stuffed Fried Bread Parcels

KHOBZ BISHEMAR

Eaten hot, straight from the griddle or frying pan, these parcels make a delicious snack. Don't be put off by the thought of the beef suet – the yeast dough is pricked before cooking so it absorbs the excess fat from filling, making it rich and tasty and moreish. It is not so good cold.

SERVES 4

1 quantity Moroccan bread dough, kneaded (see page 110)
butter, for frying
salt

FOR THE FILLING:

75 g/3 oz beef suet, finely chopped
1 dried red chilli, finely chopped
3 tbsp finely chopped onion
3 tbsp finely chopped fresh parsley
½ tsp ground cumin
1 tsp paprika

With lightly oiled hands, form the dough into four balls then flatten each to a rectangle about 30 x 20 cm/12 x 8 in.

In a bowl, mix together the filling ingredients. Spread one quarter of the mixture along the centre of each dough rectangle, then fold one long side over the filling. Fold over the other long side. Flatten each rectangle to 30 x 20 cm/12 x 8 in, then fold again as above. Transfer to a buttered baking sheet, cover and leave to rise.

Heat a griddle or heavy frying pan and add a small knob of butter. Using a fork, prick the dough parcels five or six times on each side. Fry the parcels for 8–10 minutes each side until crisp and golden. Serve hot, brushed lightly with extra melted butter, if liked.

RIGHT *The Sahara desert, Algeria*

Egg-filled Tunisian Fried Pastries

——————— BRIKS A L'OEUF ———————

*Serve these light crisp Tunisian pastries immediately they are cooked, and take
care that the egg does not trickle down your chin.
Although not authentic, Chinese spring roll wrappers make a useful alternative
to the traditional* warka *pastry, which may be hard to obtain.*

MAKES 4

20 g/¾ oz butter
3–4 spring onions, finely
   chopped
1 tbsp chopped fresh
   parsley
115 g/4 oz canned tuna,
   drained and mashed
a few capers, chopped

1 tbsp freshly grated
   Parmesan cheese, if liked
salt and pepper
4 warka leaves or Chinese
   spring roll wrappers
4 small eggs
1 egg white, lightly beaten
oil for frying
lemon wedges, to serve

Melt the butter in a pan, then add the spring onions
and gently cook until softened. Then mix in the
parsley, tuna, capers, cheese if used, and salt and
pepper. Leave to cool.

Spread out the *warka* leaves or spring roll
wrappers and place a quarter of the filling on one
half of each. Break an egg over each portion of
filling. Fold over the pastry or wrapper to cover the
filling and firmly seal the edges with egg white,
giving the edges a double fold for an extra firm seal.

Heat a 2.5 cm/1 in depth of oil in a large frying pan
until hot but not smoking. Slide in the *briks,* baste
the top with hot oil and fry until the undersides are
browned. Turn over and fry the other side.

Drain quickly on paper towels and serve with
lemon wedges.

Grated Carrot Salad

*A less piquant version of this spicy salad can be made by omitting the cinnamon,
ginger and honey, and adding 3 tbsp lemon juice, and sugar, orange-flower
water and salt to taste.*

SERVES 4

450 g/1 lb small carrots,
   coarsely grated
1–2 tbsp clear honey
juice of 1 lemon

5 tbsp olive oil
1 tsp ground cinnamon
½ tsp ground ginger
75 g/3 oz raisins
salt and pepper

Put the grated carrot into a large bowl. In a small
bowl, mix together the remaining ingredients then
pour the mixture over the carrots and stir well. Leave
for 1 hour before serving.

Carrot Dip

OMI HOURIYA

This spicy homely Tunisian purée is served cold as a dip for bread. Although not traditional, I sometimes also serve it with grilled meats and poultry.

SERVES 4

675 g/1½ lb carrots
   chopped
2 garlic cloves, chopped
2 tbsp olive oil
½ small onion, very finely
   chopped

2 tsp ground cumin
1–2 tbsp lemon juice
about 1 tsp Harissa (see
   page 120)
salt

Cook the carrots and garlic in a pan of boiling water until the carrots are tender. Drain.

Meanwhile, heat the oil in a large pan, add the onion and cook until softened. Add the cumin and heat gently until fragrant. Add the carrots, garlic, and remaining ingredients to taste. Remove from the heat, mash together. Leave to cool.

Aubergine Purée

───────── SALATAT ASWAD ─────────

*This delicious aubergine and tomato mixture is typical of the purée dishes which
are called salads in North Africa and the Middle East. Serve it as a dip with
oven-warmed pitta bread or sticks of crunchy vegetables such as celery and
cucumber. It also makes a tasty accompaniment to grilled meats,
poultry and fish.*

SERVES 4
900 g/2 lb aubergines
2 garlic cloves, sliced
3 tomatoes, peeled, seeded
*   and chopped*

1 tsp paprika
½ tsp ground cumin
1 tbsp chopped coriander
1½ tbsp olive oil
3 tbsp lemon juice

Preheat the oven to 220°C/425°F/gas 7. Cut slits in
the aubergines and insert slices of garlic. Bake in the
oven until the skin is charred and blistered. Remove
from the oven and leave to cool.

Peel the aubergine, squeeze out and discard the
juices, then place in a bowl and mash with the
aubergine and garlic, tomatoes, paprika, cumin,
coriander and salt.

Heat the oil in a frying pan, add the aubergine
mixture and fry, stirring frequently, until very thick;
this will take about 15 minutes. Pour off the excess
oil. Add lemon juice to the purée, to taste. Serve
warm or cool.

LEFT Top *Pumpkin Purée,*
Middle *Aubergine Purée,*
Below *Carrot Dip*

Pumpkin Purée

───────── AJLOUKE ET POTIRON ─────────

*Tunisian Harissa and other spices transform pumpkin into a characterful dish
that is eaten cold with bread. Reserve the liquid from the pumpkin to use in
soups or casseroles.*

SERVES 4
675 g/1½ lb piece
*   pumpkin*
¾ tsp caraway seeds
¾ tsp ground coriander
1½ tbsp olive oil

1 plump garlic clove,
*   crushed*
about ¼ tsp Harissa (see
*   page 120)*
2–3 tbsp lemon juice
salt

Peel the pumpkin and remove the seeds and threads.
Chop the flesh and cook gently in a little water in a
covered pan until tender. Drain thoroughly.

In a large pan, gently heat the oil, add the caraway
seeds and coriander, stirring occasionally until
fragrant. Then add the pumpkin, garlic, *Harissa*,
lemon juice and salt. Remove the pan from the heat,
mash all the ingredients together, then leave to cool.

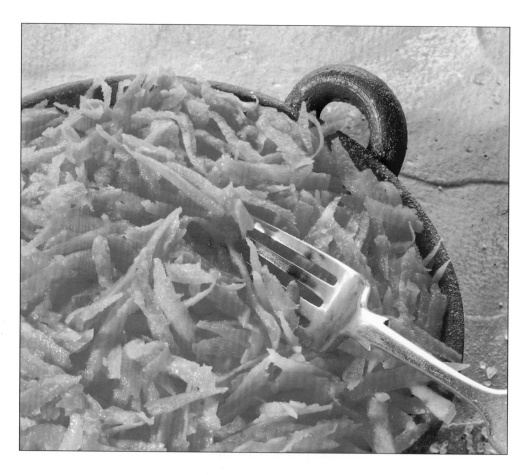

Orange and Carrot Salad

The flavours of oranges and carrots have a natural affinity, each one enhancing the other. They are often combined in soup, but here they are used to make tasty salad.

SERVES 4

450 g/1 lb carrots, peeled and coarsely grated
juice of 1 orange
juice of 1 lemon
1–2 tbsp orange-flower water
salt and icing sugar

In a large bowl, mix together the carrots, orange and lemon juices and orange-flower water. Add salt and icing sugar to taste. Cover and chill.

Parsley, Onion and Lemon Salad

This sharp, fresh-tasting Moroccan salad makes a good accompaniment to grilled oily fish such as sardines, or it can be used, together with some olive oil, to marinate the fish before cooking.

SERVES 4

1–1½ *bunches parsley,
coarsely chopped*
1 *large Spanish onion,
thinly sliced*

4 *large lemons, preferably
thin-skinned, peeled and
diced*
salt and pepper

In a large bowl, toss all the ingredients together, then cover and chill lightly.

31

Tunisian Egg and Aubergine Tagine

TAGINE BETINJAL

In this dish, it is important not to cook the aubergine mixture after the eggs and cheese have been added otherwise they will become tough and the fat will seep unappetisingly out of the cheese.

SERVES 4

450 g/1 lb aubergines, diced
salt and pepper
oil for shallow frying
1 onion, coarsely chopped
2 garlic cloves, chopped
3 eggs, lightly beaten

1 hard-boiled egg, quite finely chopped
bunch of mixed coriander and parsley, finely chopped
50 g/2 oz Gruyere cheese, grated

Sprinkle the aubergines with salt and leave to drain for 30–60 minutes. Rinse well under running cold water then dry on paper towels.

Heat a little oil in a *tagine* or heavy frying pan, add the onion and cook until soft. Add more oil. When it is hot add the aubergines until they are soft and lightly coloured. Stir in the garlic and cook, stirring, until it becomes fragrant. Remove from the heat.

In a bowl, mix together the remaining ingredients, then stir into the aubergine mixture. Over a very low heat, cook gently for about 10 minutes until just set, then brown under a hot grill, if liked.

ABOVE *Water pump and well at Kerzas, Tunisia*

Baked Aubergines with Cheese

———— BATINGAN BI JIBN ————

Serve this appetizing Arab dish warm, as a first course or a light main course accompanied by salad and pitta bread.

SERVES 4
2 aubergines
2 tsp dried mint
2 tomatoes, peeled, seeded
   and chopped

1 garlic clove, chopped
pepper
350 g/12 oz goat's cheese

Preheat the grill. Place the aubergines in a grill pan, then grill them, turning regularly until the skin is charred and blistered. Preheat the oven to 200°C/ 400°F/gas 6.

When the aubergines are cool enough to handle, peel them and chop the flesh. Transfer to a bowl, then add the mint, tomatoes, garlic and pepper and mix together. Spoon the mixture into a baking dish and crumble the goat's cheese over the top. Bake for about 25 minutes, until the cheese is melted and lightly browned.

Cooked Vegetable Salad

———— SALADE DE ZAALOUK ————

This salad from Tunisia is quite spicy-hot. It can be kept, covered, for 2–3 days in the refrigerator; indeed, it tastes better if the flavours are given time to mature and mellow.

SERVES 4–6
3 tbsp olive oil
1 onion, chopped
4 courgettes, sliced
2 aubergines, cubed
2–3 garlic cloves, crushed
4 red peppers, sliced

2 fresh chillies, chopped
4 well-flavoured tomatoes,
   peeled and chopped
salt and pepper
parsley or coriander, to
   garnish, if liked

Heat the oil in a pan, then add the onion, courgettes, aubergines and garlic and cook for about 10 minutes. Add the peppers, chillies and tomatoes, season and cook gently, stirring occasionally, until the vegetables are tender and there is no free liquid.

Transfer to a bowl and leave to cool. Garnish with parsley or coriander, if liked.

Chicken Strips with Mint

These delicately marinated chicken strips are threaded onto skewers before being grilled or barbecued. Spearmint (the variety of mint most often used) is popular fresh and dried; usually it is home-dried in the hot sun then before using, the dried leaves are rubbed between the hands until the warmth releases the flavoursome essential oils.

SERVES 4

2 tbsp lemon juice

1½ tsp olive oil

2 tbsp chopped fresh mint, or 1 tbsp dried mint

2 garlic cloves, finely chopped

salt and pepper

400 g/14 oz skinless chicken breast, cut across the grain into 1.25 cm/ ½ in thick slices

lettuce leaves and tomato wedges, to garnish

In a large shallow dish, combine the lemon juice, olive oil, mint, garlic and seasonings. Add the chicken, turn to coat with the lemon mixture, cover and leave for up to 2 hours in a cool larder, or up to 8 hours in the refrigerator. Bring into room temperature 30 minutes before cooking.

If using wooden skewers, soak 4 or 5 15 cm/6 in skewers in water for 30 minutes. Thread the pieces of chicken onto the skewers, then cook under or on a preheated grill, or barbecue for 2½–3½ minutes each side. Serve on a bed of lettuce, garnished with tomato wedges.

LEFT *El Djem, Tunisia*

Grilled Keftas

It is generally recommended that the lamb used for Keftas should contain about ten percent fat, to bind the ingredients together and keep them moist during cooking. Leaner meat can be used, however, if you do not mind crumblier, slightly drier Keftas.

SERVES 4

600 g/1¼ lb lamb, freshly minced
1 onion, grated
1 tbsp paprika
1 tsp ground cumin
¼ tsp ground cinnamon
¼ tsp cayenne pepper

1 bunch of coriander, chopped
several mint leaves, chopped
2 tbsp water
2 tbsp olive oil
1 egg, beaten
salt and pepper
salt and cumin, mixed, to serve

Mix all the ingredients together then knead well to make a homogenous paste; this may take 15 minutes. Chill for 1 hour.

Preheat the grill or barbecue. Form the meat mixture into small cakes about 5 cm/2 in diameter and 2 cm/¾ in thick. Grill or barbecue for a few minutes each side. Serve sprinkled with a mixture of salt and cumin.

Kebabs

Kebabs are one of the most famous dishes of the Arab world. Lamb is almost invariably used, and traditionally it is not interspersed with vegetables on the skewer as this would affect the cooking of the meat. Instead of marinating the raw lamb, the kebabs are sometimes sprinkled with spices after cooking.

SERVES 4

675 g/1½ lb lean lamb, cubed
chopped fresh parsley and lemon wedges, to serve

FOR THE MARINADE:
4 tbsp olive oil
1 tbsp lemon juice
1 onion, grated
1 garlic clove, finely chopped
1½ tsp ground cumin
1½ tsp cayenne pepper
2 tbsp finely chopped fresh parsley
salt and pepper

Mix together all the marinade ingredients. Thread the lamb onto skewers and lay in a shallow non-metallic dish. Pour over the marinade. Leave for at least 2 hours in a cool place, turning occasionally.

Preheat the grill or barbecue. Grill or barbecue the kebabs, turning occasionally, for 4–7 minutes, depending on how well cooked you like the meat. Serve sprinkled with parsley and accompanied by lemon wedges.

LEFT *Grilled* Keftas

Fried Peppers with Capers and Garlic

The essential character of this pepper dish comes from the slightly charred taste of the peppers which are fried till their skins are scorched. The dish can be served hot as a vegetable accompaniment, or chilled as a first course.

SERVES 4–6

4 tbsp olive oil
800 g/1¾ lb red peppers,
   cut into strips

4 garlic cloves, sliced
1 tbsp salt-packed capers
2 tbsp white wine vinegar
salt and pepper

Heat the oil in a frying pan until it is quite hot, then fry the peppers, stirring frequently, until they are charred around the edges. Add the garlic and capers. Cook until they sizzle, then stir in the vinegar and seasoning; because of the salt in the capers little additional salt will be necessary.

Allow the vinegar to evaporate for a minute or so, then either serve immediately, or leave to cool, cover, chill and serve cold.

Beetroot Salad

If you buy ready-cooked beetroot, make sure they have not been preserved in vinegar.

SERVES 4–6

900 g/2 lb beetroot
¼ Spanish onion, finely
   chopped
1 tbsp finely chopped
   parsley

2 tbsp lemon juice
6 tbsp olive oil
pinch of chilli pepper
salt and pepper

Cook the unpeeled beetroot in a pan of boiling water until tender. Drain and remove the skins under cold running water. Dice the beetroot, place in a bowl, then mix with the onion and parsley.

In a small bowl, whisk together the lemon juice, oil, chilli pepper and seasoning. Pour over the vegetables, toss lightly, cover and chill.

RIGHT *Fried Peppers with Capers and Garlic*

Orange Salad

*Oranges in North Africa, especially Morocco, are wonderfully sweet and juicy.
They are used to make many different refreshing salads for serving at the
beginning of meals and at the end.*

SERVES 6–8

6 ripe oranges, peeled and
thinly sliced horizontally
12 fresh dates, stoned and
thinly sliced

12 blanched almonds,
slivered
1–2 tbsp orange-flower
water
ground cinnamon for
sprinkling

Place the orange slices on a shallow serving plate.
Scatter over the dates and almonds and sprinkle over
orange-flower water. Finally, sprinkle with ground
cinnamon. Cover and chill lightly.

Grilled Red Pepper and Tomato Dip

— SALATA MECHOUIA NABLIA —

This roast vegetable salad comes from Nabeul, in Tunisia.

SERVES 4–6

450 g/1 lb large red
peppers
1 fresh red chilli
2–4 garlic cloves, unpeeled
3 well-flavoured tomatoes
1 tbsp caraway seeds

2–3 tbsp olive oil
salt
quarters of hard-boiled
egg, chunks of canned
tuna and black olives, to
serve

Preheat the grill and place the peppers, chilli, garlic
and tomatoes in a grill pan and cook, turning
occasionally until the skins are charred and blistered,
and the garlic is soft. Leave to cool then peel the
vegetables. Discard the cores and seeds from the
peppers and chilli, and the seeds from the tomatoes.
Put all the vegetables into a blender or food
processor, or through a sieve.

In a frying pan, gently heat the caraway seeds and
oil until fragrant. Add to the blender or food
processor with the salt and whizz to a purée. Chill
before serving. Serve in a bowl with quarters of
hard-boiled eggs, chunks of canned tuna and black
olives around it.

Eggs poached on Pepper and Tomato Ragout

———— CHACKOUKA ————

The inclusion of fiery-hot red chillies pinpoints this as a Tunisian dish.

SERVES 4

3 tbsp olive oil
1 large onion, thinly sliced
350 g/12 oz red peppers,
 sliced
1–2 fresh red chillies,
 seeded and chopped

675 g/1½ lb well-
 flavoured firm but ripe
 tomatoes, peeled, seeded
 and chopped
salt and pepper
pinch of sugar, if liked
4 eggs

Heat the oil in a deep heavy frying or sauté pan, then cook the onion until softened and beginning to colour. Add the peppers and chillies and cook, stirring occasionally, until almost soft. Stir in the tomatoes and cook for a further 8 minutes or so until all the vegetables are soft but not mushy. Add salt and pepper, and a little sugar, if necessary.

Make 4 deep depressions in the pepper mixture, break in the eggs, cover and pan and cook gently until the eggs are cooked as you like them, basting once or twice with the juices. Serve immediately.

Potato Omelette

———— MAACOUDA BIL BATATA ————

This herb-speckled omelette has similar ingredients to the Spanish tortilla *but the potatoes are mashed rather than sliced. Serve it as a substantial snack, or a light lunch accompanied by a green salad. It is good eaten cold as well as warm, and makes a wonderful picnic food.*

SERVES 4

350 g/12 oz potatoes,
 chopped
1 Spanish onion, chopped
3 tbsp olive oil
2 garlic cloves, chopped
4 eggs

1 tsp Harissa (see
 page 120)
1 bunch of mixed coriander
 and parsley, finely
 chopped
salt

Cook the potatoes in a pan of boiling water until tender. Meanwhile, heat 2 tbsp oil in a frying pan and fry the onion, until soft and lightly browned. Stir in the garlic and cook, stirring, until fragrant.

Drain the potatoes and return to the saucepan. Over a low heat, mash the potatoes, then stir in the onions and garlic. Remove from the heat.

In a mixing bowl, lightly whisk the eggs with the *Harissa,* herbs and salt. Gradually beat the egg mixture into the potatoes.

Heat the remaining oil in a large heavy frying pan, add the egg and potato mixture and cook over a very low heat until the bottom has set. Brown the top under a hot grill.

Dried Broad Bean Dip

BYESAR

Byesar is close to the hearts of North Africans, and many crave it when they are abroad. Dried broad beans are the usual main ingredient but in Tangier split green peas and spring onions may be used. In another variation, the beans are cooked with cabbage and flavoured with paprika, cumin, garlic and salt, while Tunisians add Harissa or paprika and a generous seasoning of cayenne. Buy skinned dried broad beans if possible. The customary way of eating Byesar is to sprinkle a piece of bread with the accompanying slices then scoop up the dip.

SERVES 4–6

225 g/8 oz skinned dried broad beans, soaked overnight and drained
3 garlic cloves
1 tsp cumin seeds
virgin olive oil
salt
Moroccan bread (see page 110) and a small bowl of mixed ground cumin, cayenne and salt, to serve

Cook the beans with the garlic and cumin in a saucepan, just covered by water for 1–2 hours (depending on the age and quality of the beans) until tender.

Drain the bean mixture reserving the liquid, then purée in a blender or by rubbing through a sieve, adding enough of the liquid and olive oil to make a smooth cream. Season with salt and transfer to an ovenproof dish.

Just before serving, warm in the oven with a little more oil trickled over the surface and sprinkled with *za'atar* or thyme, marjoram or oregano. Serve with Moroccan bread and a small bowl of mixed ground cumin, cayenne and salt.

3
Fish

With its curved coastline, North Africa has access to many fishing grounds both in the Mediterranean Sea and the colder Atlantic Ocean. Tunisia lands the richest and most diverse catches because its coast has one of the Mediterranean's widest areas of continental shelf, which is where the fish flourish. The commonest catches are red mullet, seabass, bream, sardines, anchovies, hake and prawns, but local specialities can be found along the coast, at Oulidia, in Morocco, for example, where you may find sea urchins, oysters and mussels on the menu.

Baked Fish filled with Stuffed Dates

*Shad are traditionally used for this Moroccan dish, but any large freshwater
fish, such as carp, can be used. Alternatively, use seabass.*

SERVES 6
175 ml/6 fl oz water
2¹/₂ tbsp ground rice
150 g/5 oz blanched
  almonds, very finely
  chopped
ground ginger
1¹/₂–2 tsp sugar
15 g/¹/₂ oz butter

450 g/1 lb plump fresh
  dates, stoned
1 shad, carp or sea bass
  weighing about 2 kg/
  4¹/₄ lb, cleaned and
  scaled
¹/₂ onion, grated
³/₄ tsp ground cinnamon

Bring the water to boil in a small saucepan, pour in
the ground rice, stirring, and return to the boil for 30
seconds. Remove from the heat, cover and leave to
cool.

Preheat the oven to 170°C/325°F/gas 3. Reserve 2
tbsp of the chopped almonds and mix the rest with
the cooled rice, ¹/₂ tsp ground ginger, 1¹/₂–2 tsp sugar,
butter and seasoning. Fill the dates with the almond
mixture.

Rub the fish with seasoning and a little ground
ginger and fill with as many stuffed dates as
possible. Put the fish on a large piece of oiled foil
placed on a baking sheet and add any remaining
dates. Sprinkle with the onion. Fold up the foil,
sealing the edges firmly together. Bake for 15
minutes per 450 g/1 lb. Increase the oven
temperature to the highest setting. Unwrap the foil
around the fish, sprinkle the fish and fruit with the
reserved nuts and the ground cinnamon and put on
the highest oven shelf until crisp and brown.

ABOVE *Pulses and nuts stall, Marrakech, Morocco*

Crisp-fried Fish

HUT MAKALLI

Small crisply fried fish are popular street food in coastal areas. The egg coating makes a protective shield around the fish, keeping it moist, and the semolina gives a good crunchy outer "jacket". Sometimes very small fish are used, even smaller than whitebait, or anchovies, small sardines or sprats or small lemon sole. Sometimes this dish is served with Chermoula (see page 126). You will need a large frying pan and you will find it easiest to cook the fish in batches.

SERVES 4
4 eggs
4 tbsp chopped fresh flat-
   leaved parsley
¼ tsp ground cumin
¼ tsp paprika
pinch of chilli powder
salt and pepper
450 g/1 lb sprats or
   whitebait, according to
   size, trimmed

fine semolina for coating
olive oil for medium-deep
   frying
lemon wedges and sprigs
   of flat-leaved parsley, to
   serve

In a mixing bowl, lightly whisk together the eggs, parsley, spices, chilli and seasoning. Season the fish, then dip in the egg mixture to coat evenly. Roll the fish lightly but evenly in semolina. Repeat the egg and semolina coatings once more.

Heat about 2.5 cm/1 in of oil in a large frying pan. When very hot, add fish in a single layer and not touching each other. Fry quickly until crisp and golden.

Drain immediately on paper towels and serve with parsley sprigs and lemon wedges.

Fried Fish

A tasty yet very simple Moroccan recipe for fried fish steaks.

SERVES 4
4 tbsp finely chopped fresh
   coriander
½ red chilli, seeded and
   finely chopped
3 garlic cloves, finely
   chopped
½ tsp ground cumin

½ tsp black pepper
juice of 1 lemon
salt
150 ml/¼ pt olive oil
1–2.25 kg/2–4½ lb fish,
   cut into 4 cm/1½ in
   steaks
semolina for coating

Mix together the coriander, chilli, garlic, spices, lemon juice, a pinch of salt and half the oil. Rub into the fish, cover and leave in a cool place for 1–2 hours.

Toss the fish in semolina to coat thoroughly but evenly. Heat the remaining oil in a large frying pan, then fry the fish in batches until golden on both sides. Serve immediately.

RIGHT *Crisp-fried Fish*

La Gaulette Grilled Sardines with Tomato Relish

Around the square at La Gaulette – a little town whose name means bottleneck, because it sits at the neck of the ship canal connecting Tunis with the sea – there is a cluster of rerstaurants specializing in fish. In summer, the tables spill far out over the pavement and the smell of a busy charcoal grill scents the atmosphere.

SERVES 4

16 fresh sardines
sprigs of coriander for
    garnish

FOR THE MARINADE:

1 garlic clove
2 tsp coriander seeds,
    toasted
1 dried red chilli, seeded
    and crushed
finely grated rind and juice
    of 1 lime
4 tbsp virgin olive oil
salt and pepper

FOR THE RELISH:

4 spring onions, white part
    only, chopped
juice of 1 lime
225 g/8 oz well-flavoured
    tomatoes, peeled, seeded
    and chopped
1 sun-dried tomato half,
    chopped
½ dried red chilli, seeded
    and chopped
3 tbsp chopped coriander

Using the back of a knife, scrape off the scales from the sardines working from tail-end to head. Using scissors, cut off the fins and cut along the stomach. Remove and discard the intestines. Wash the fish thoroughly and pat dry with paper towels. Lay the sardines in a shallow non-metallic dish.

Pound the garlic and coriander with a pinch of salt and the crushed chilli. Add the lime rind and juice, then gradually work in the oil. Pour over the sardines, turn to coat with the mixture, then cover and leave for about 1 hour in a cool place, turning two or three times. Mix the relish ingredients together in a food processor or blender.

Lift the sardines from the dish, reserving the spice mixture. Cook the sardines in a grill pan under a preheated grill for 2–3 minutes a side, basting with the marinade. Serve garnished with lime slices.

Algerian Grilled Sardines with Lemon and Coriander

This particular recipe comes from an ex-patriot Algerian living in France.

SERVES 4

6 tbsp olive oil
3 tbsp lemon juice
2 tbsp chopped fresh
    coriander
good pinch of paprika

good pinch of cumin
salt and pepper
900 g/2 lb prepared fresh
    sardines (see above for
    cleaning sardines)

LEFT *La Gaulette Grilled
Sardines with Tomato Relish*

Mix together the oil, lemon juice, coriander and seasoning. Lay the sardines in a single layer in a large, shallow dish and pour over the oil mixture. Leave in a cool place for 1 hour, turning the sardines 2 or 3 times.

Preheat the grill. Grill the sardines for 2–3 minutes a side, brushing with the lemon mixture as the fish browns and when turning them. Serve with any remaining lemon mixture poured over.

Bream with Preserved Lemons in Oil

———— DAURADE AUX CITRONS CONFITS ————

Daurade is the gilt-head bream, which is considered the star of the sea bream family, but if you are unable to find it use dentex or common sea bream for this Algerian dish.

SERVES 4

16–20 slices Lemons Preserved in Oil (see page 124)

1 bream, preferably gilt-head, weighing about 1.5 kg/3¼ lb, or other firm white fish, cleaned and scaled

150 ml/¼ pt oil from the jar of lemons

1 tbsp chopped fresh coriander

1 tbsp paprika

salt and pepper

Lay about 12 lemon slices in the bottom of a large shallow baking dish. Make several slashes along each side of the fish, season inside and out, put the coriander inside and rub the outside with paprika. Put the fish on the Preserved Lemon slices and cover with more lemon slices.

Pour over the oil and bake the fish in an oven preheated to its hottest setting for about 5 minutes. Baste the fish, lower the oven temperature to about 180°C/350°F/gas 4 and bake for a further 40 minutes or so, basting occasionally.

Tunisian Grilled Prawns

*Cooking this dish evokes memories of the evening sky in the sleepy Tunisian
fishing village of Bizerta, the sounds of night drawing in, and the exotic aroma
of charcoal grilled prawns wafting tantalizingly past my nose.*

SERVES 4

450 g/1 lb raw king
   prawns in their shells
2 garlic cloves, crushed
4 tbsp olive oil
1 tsp ground cumin
½ tsp ground ginger

1 tsp paprika
¼ tsp cayenne pepper
the leaves from 1 bunch of
   coriander, finely chopped
salt
lemon wedges, to serve

Remove the heads and legs from the prawns. Using
kitchen scissors, cut the prawns in half lengthways,
leaving the tails intact. Lay the prawns in a single
layer in a large, shallow dish.

In a small bowl, mix together the remaining
ingredients, except the lemon wedges, then pour the
spice mixture over the prawns and leave in a cool
place for 1–2 hours, turning the prawns occasionally.

Preheat the grill. Grill the prawns for 3–4 minutes
until they turn pink, brushing with any remaining
marinade as they cook. Serve with lemon wedges.

Almond Coated Baked Fish

—————— HUT BENOUA ——————

The Moroccan fishing port of Safi is the home of this unusual but delicious fish dish with its crisp sweet, spiced coating.

SERVES 4

225 g/8 oz blanched
  almonds, toasted and
  ground
65 g/2½ oz icing sugar
1 tbsp orange-flower water
1 tbsp ground cinnamon
100 ml/3½ fl oz water
50 g/2 oz butter, softened,
  plus extra for buttering

salt and pepper
1 seabass or bream
  weighing about 1.75 kg/
  4 lb, cleaned
1 onion, finely chopped
pinch of saffron threads,
  crushed

Preheat the oven to 190°C/375°F/gas 5. Put the almonds, icing sugar, orange-flower water, cinnamon, 3 tbsp water, half the butter, and seasoning in a bowl and mix to a smooth paste. Season the fish inside and out then fill with half the almond mixture.

Mix the onion, saffron and remaining water together and pour into a large buttered baking dish. Put the fish on the onion mixture and spread the remaining almond mixture over the fish. Melt the remaining butter and trickle over the almond mixture.

Bake for about 45 minutes until the fish is cooked and the almond topping has a crust on it yet is still soft underneath.

Marinated Fish cooked in Spiced Oil

—————— POISSON EN TAJINE MQUALLI ——————

Halibut can be replaced by hake, cod or grey mullet in this recipe.

SERVES 4-6

900 g/2 lb halibut steaks
175 ml/6 fl oz olive oil
1 tsp ground ginger
pinch of saffron threads,
  crushed
stoned black olives and
  lemon quarters, to
  garnish

FOR THE MARINADE:

3 garlic cloves
salt
1 tsp cayenne pepper
1 tsp ground coriander
1 tsp cumin

To make the marinade, crush the garlic with a large pinch of salt then mix with the spices. Rub each halibut with the marinade then put in a single layer in a heavy baking dish and leave in a cool place for 6 hours. Preheat the oven to 190°C/375°F/gas 5.

Mix the oil with the saffron and ginger. Pour over the fish, cover and bake for about 20–25 minutes until the fish flakes easily. Serve garnished with olives and lemons.

RIGHT *Almond Coated Baked Fish*

Small Fish Balls with Tomato Sauce

———— COUIRAT EL HOUT ————

Fish balls are a favourite dish all along the coast of North Africa. The fish used varies according to what is available. Sometimes the balls are fried, sometimes, as in this Algerian recipe, they are cooked in a sauce.

SERVES 4–6

2 slices of bread, crusts removed, presoaked in a little water

675 g/1½ lb fillet of firm white fish such as hake, haddock or cod, skinned and minced

1 large egg, lightly whisked

1 bunch of parsley, chopped

salt and pepper

FOR THE SAUCE:

1 Spanish onion finely chopped

3 tbsp olive oil

2 garlic cloves, finely chopped

3 large well-flavoured tomatoes, peeled, seeded and chopped

½ red pepper, finely chopped

1 tsp each ground cumin and paprika

pinch of cayenne pepper

300 ml/½ pt water

salt and pepper

chopped flat-leaved parsley or coriander, to garnish

Squeeze the bread dry, place in a large mixing bowl, add the other ingredients and seasoning and mix thoroughly. With wet hands, form into balls about the size of walnuts.

To make the sauce, heat the oil in a frying pan, then add the onion and cook until softened. Add the garlic and red pepper, cook for 2–3 minutes then stir in the spices followed by the tomatoes and water. Bring to the boil. Skim the froth from the surface, add the fish balls and simmer gently for about 8 minutes, turning once.

Transfer the fish balls to a warm serving dish and keep warm. Boil the sauce hard until lightly thickened. Pour over the fish balls and sprinkle with chopped parsley or coriander.

ABOVE *Coastline at Medique, Morocco*

Fish Tagine with Chermoula

There are many different versions of this dish, so feel free to change the ingredients given here to suit your taste.

SERVES 4
675 g/1½ lb grey mullet,
   bream or monkfish fillets

FOR THE MARINADE:
3 tbsp olive oil
3 garlic cloves, crushed
1½ tsp ground cumin
1 tsp paprika

1 fresh green chilli, finely
   chopped
1 handful of fresh
   coriander leaves, finely
   chopped
4 tbsp lemon juice
salt
lemon wedges, to serve

Place the fish in a shallow non-metallic dish. Mix together the marinade ingredients in a small bowl, then pour over the fish, cover and leave in a cool place 3–4 hours, turning occasionally.

Preheat the grill, then place the fish in a grill pan and grill for about 4 minutes each side, depending on the thickness, basting with the coriander mixture occasionally, until the flesh flakes when tested with the point of a sharp knife. Serve warm with lemon wedges.

Fish and Celery Tagine

—————— HUT BIL KARFAS ——————

Here, celery stalks serve the function of the bamboo canes in Fish Tagine with Olives, as well as adding flavour to the fish and sauce.

SERVES 4
450 g/1 lb celery stalks.
2 garlic cloves
salt
2 tsp paprika
1 tsp ground cumin
pinch of saffron threads,
   toasted and crushed
pinch of cayenne pepper
2½ tbsp olive oil
1.5 kg/3¼ lb firm white
   fish such as bream or
   bass, cleaned

lemon juice
350 g/12 oz well-flavoured
   tomatoes, peeled, seeded
   and chopped
½ Preserved Lemon in salt
   (see page 125), pulp
   removed if liked, the peel
   chopped
1 tsp chopped parsley

Mix the garlic, salt, spices and oil in a spice grinder. With the point of a sharp knife, cut 4 diagonal slashes on each side of the fish. Rub the spice mixture into the cavity and on both sides of the fish, pressing well into the slashes. Lay the fish on a plate and spread over any remaining spice mixture. Leave in a cool place, but not the refrigerator, for 1 hour. Preheat the oven to 190°C/375°F/gas 5.

Cut the celery stalks in half lengthways, then cut across into 5 cm/2 in pieces. Arrange in a single layer in a large baking dish. Put the fish on the celery. Scrape any spice mixture off the plate and spread over the fish. Cover with the tomatoes, Preserved Lemon peel and parsley. Cover with foil and bake for 30 minutes. Uncover and bake for a further 15 minutes or so.

Red Mullet with Red Pepper and Mint Sauce

———— ROUGET AU POIVRE ROUGE ————

Mint gives an unusual flavour to the red pepper sauce which is poured over these pretty and delicious little fish.

SERVES 4

1½–2 tbsp olive oil
4 red mullet, about 225 g/
  8 oz each, cleaned and
  scaled
salt and pepper
1 onion, finely chopped
2 garlic cloves, chopped

1 small red pepper,
  charred and skinned if
  liked, then seeded and
  chopped
pinch of cayenne pepper
3–5 mint leaves
small sprig of thyme
2–3 tbsp lemon juice

Season the mullet then fry it in the olive oil for 4–5 minutes each side, until the flesh flakes easily. Drain on paper towels then transfer to a warm plate and keep warm. Add the onion, garlic and pepper to the pan and fry gently until the onion is soft and beginning to colour. Stir in the cayenne pepper, thyme, mint, lemon juice and salt and boil until slightly reduced. Discard the thyme sprig, pour the sauce over the fish and serve immediately.

Fish Tagine with Lemons and Olives

———— HUT BIL ZEETOON ————

For this tagine, bamboo canes are traditionally laid in a lattice pattern in the bottom of the dish to prevent the fish sticking, but when the dish is cooked in the oven, it does not matter if the canes are omitted.

SERVES 4

1 quantity Chermoula 2
  (see page 126)
1 firm white fish weighing
  about 1.5 kg/3¼ lb,
  cleaned

350 g/12 oz cracked green
  olives
2 limes, peeled and sliced
3 tbsp olive oil, if liked
3 tbsp lime juice, if liked

Rub half the *Chermoula* into the skin and cavity of the fish. Leave in a cool place for 1 hour.

Blanch the olives in three separate changes of water, then drain well and mix with the remaining *Chermoula*. Preheat the oven to 200°C/400°F/gas 6.

If liked, make a lattice pattern with bamboo canes in the bottom of a baking dish large enough to hold the fish. Alternatively, oil the baking dish. Lay the fish in the dish, and cover with the lime slices then the olives. Pour the olive oil, if liked, and a little water around the fish, cover the dish with foil and bake for about 35 minutes. Uncover and bake for a further 10–15 minutes. Sprinkle with lime juice, if liked. Serve with the cooking juices spooned over.

LEFT *Red Mullet with Red Pepper and Mint Sauce*

Fish Tagine with Peppers, Potatoes and Tomatoes

———— HUT TUNGERA ————

Hut tungera makes a flavoursome, substantial fish dish.

SERVES 4

1 quantity Chermoula 1
  or 2 (see pages 126)
4 fish cutlets or steaks cut
  across the fish, total
  weight 1 kg/2¼ lb
2 potatoes, thinly sliced

3 tomatoes, sliced
2 red peppers, sliced
1 tbsp tomato purée
1 garlic clove, chopped
4 tbsp lemon juice
4 tbsp olive oil
5 tbsp water

Rub some of the *Chermoula* into the fish and leave in a cool place, but not the refrigerator, for 1 hour. Preheat the oven to 190°C/375°F/gas 5.

If liked, lay bamboo canes in a lattice pattern in the bottom of a baking dish. Alternatively, oil the baking dish. Place the fish in the dish and cover with the potatoes. Spread with a little *Chermoula,* then cover with the tomatoes and peppers.

Mix the remaining *Chermoula* with the tomato purée, garlic, lemon juice, oil and water. Pour over the fish, cover with foil and bake for 25 minutes. Uncover and bake for a further 10–15 minutes. Allow to cool slightly, and serve warm.

Fish Baked with Preserved Lemons, Eggs and Onions

Spiced eggs may seem rather unusual stuffing for fish, but they are typically Moroccan, and surprisingly delicious.

SERVES 4

5 tbsp oil
300 g/10 oz red onions,
  finely chopped
50 g/2 oz butter
2 eggs
2 tbsp chopped fresh
  coriander
pinch of saffron threads,
  toasted and crushed

1 Preserved Lemon in salt
  (see page 125), pulp
  removed, the peel thinly
  sliced
salt and pepper
1 kg/2¼ lb white fish
  fillets
chopped fresh parsley, to
  garnish

Preheat the oven to 190°C/375°F/gas 5. Heat 2 tbsp oil in a frying pan and cook the onion until soft and transparent. Meanwhile in another pan, melt half the butter and fry the eggs until almost set, then stir them like scrambled eggs until set.

Stir the eggs, coriander, saffron, Preserved Lemon peel and seasoning into the onion.

Lay half the fish fillets, skin-side down, in a large baking dish, season and cover with half the onion mixture. Cover with the remaining fish, skin side up, and then cover with the rest of the onion mixture. Pour over the oil and dot with the butter. Bake for about 35 minutes then place the dish under a hot grill to brown the top. Sprinkle with parsley and serve.

4
Poultry

In lands where meat is in short supply, poultry often plays an important part in people's diet, especially in poorer households. The unimpressively scrawny appearance of many North African poultry usually belies their flavour; local cooks know that the best way to cook this kind of bird is to braise it slowly, until the flesh is coaxed to fall away from the bones. Pigeons are used in the great Moroccan pie, *b'stilla,* as well as in other traditional North African dishes.

Chicken Tagine with Olives and Preserved Lemons

DJEJ EMSHMEL/DJEJ MQUALLI

The recipe cannot be made with fresh lemons – if it is, it will be an entirely different dish. The mellow flavour of the preserved lemons is beautifully complemented by pinky-brown Moroccan olives.

SERVES 4

2–3 tbsp olive oil

1 Spanish onion, chopped finely

3 garlic cloves

salt and pepper

¾ tsp ground ginger

1½ tsp ground cinnamon

large pinch of saffron threads, toasted and crushed

1 chicken weighing about 1.6 kg/3½ lb

700 ml/1¼ pt chicken stock or water

115 g/4 oz greeny-brown Moroccan olives, rinsed (or Greek kalamata olives)

1 large bunch of coriander, finely chopped

1 large bunch parsley, finely chopped

1 Preserved Lemon in salt (see page 125), flesh discarded if liked, rinsed and chopped

LEFT *Chicken* Tagine *with Olives and Preserved Lemons*

Heat the oil in a pan. Fry the onion until golden. Meanwhile, in a mortar, crush the garlic with a pinch of salt then work in the ginger, cinnamon, saffron and a little pepper. Stir into the onions, cook until fragrant, then spread over the chicken.

Put the chicken in a heavy saucepan or flameproof casserole so it fits snugly, add the stock or water and bring just to simmering point. Cover and simmer very gently for about 1¼ hours, turning the chicken 2 or 3 times.

Add the olives, Preserved Lemon and herbs, cover again and cook for a further 15 minutes or so until the chicken is very tender. Taste the sauce – if the flavour needs to be more concentrated, transfer the chicken to a warm shallow serving dish, cover and keep warm, then reduce the cooking juices to a rich sauce. Tilt the pan and skim off surplus fat, if liked, then pour over the chicken.

Chicken with Grapes

DJEJ BIL EINAB

Squeezing the juice from fresh ginger is not a typically Moroccan practice but it adds a fresh note to this recipe.

SERVES 4

3.75 cm/1½ in fresh ginger

1 tsp ground cinnamon

4 chicken portions

2 tbsp unsalted butter

1 tbsp olive oil

225 g/8 oz green seedless grapes, halved

Squeeze the ginger in a garlic press to extract the juice, then mix with the cinnamon. Rub into the chicken and leave in a cool place for 2 hours.

Heat the butter and oil in a frying pan, then cook the chicken until evenly browned. Add the grapes, cover and cook gently, turning the chicken occasionally, until it is tender.

Chicken Stuffed with Couscous, with Spiced Honey Sauce

—————— DJEJ M'AHMAR ——————

This meltingly tender chicken with its almondy couscous stuffing and spiced honey sauce, is served at feasts and celebrations in Morocco. Even though the sauce contains honey, traditionally the stuffing is sweetened with generous amounts of sugar. If you would like to try sweetened stuffing, I suggest starting with a 1–1½ tbsp sugar to see if you like it. Stuffing that will not go into the bird can be put heated in the top part of a couscousier or colander put over the saucepan towards the end of cooking.

SERVES 4

1 large chicken
1½ Spanish onions, finely chopped
3 tbsp oil
2 garlic cloves, chopped
2 tsp ground cinnamon
½ tsp saffron threads, crushed
¼–½ tsp ground ginger
salt
about 570 ml/1 pt water
about 2 tbsp clear honey

FOR THE STUFFING:

about 570 ml/1 pt water
350 g/12 oz pre-cooked couscous (see page 11)
3 tbsp raisins
75 g/3 oz blanched almonds, toasted and chopped
1½ tbsp orange-flower water
2 tbsp oil
1 tsp cinnamon
pinch of ground cloves
pinch of freshly grated nutmeg
salt and pepper

Stir the water into the *couscous* and leave for 5 minutes, stirring occasionally, until the water has been absorbed. Stir in the remaining ingredients.

Loosely fill the cavity of the chicken with some of the stuffing and pack some more in the neck end. Fold over the neck flap and secure with string or a skewer. Tie up the cavity with string. Heat the oil in a saucepan just large enough to hold the chicken, then gently cook the onions until softened. Stir in the garlic, spices and salt, then add the chicken to the pan. Pour in the water, cover, bring to the boil then poach for about 30 minutes. Add the honey and continue to cook for a further 45–60 minutes or until the chicken is very tender.

Remove the chicken to a warm serving plate. Taste the sauce and boil if necessary to concentrate the flavour. Spoon any separate stuffing onto the plate and pour the sauce over the bird and stuffing.

Chicken with Chickpeas, Lemon and Parsley

———— SFERIA ————

In this Algerian dish the sauce is thickened with grated onion, parsley and
coriander, and flavoured with saffron and lemon juice.

SERVES 4

2 garlic cloves, crushed
salt and pepper
½ tsp ground ginger
pinch of saffron threads
65 g/2½ oz softened
* unsalted butter*
1 chicken weighing about
* 1.5 kg/3¼ lb*
1 cinnamon stick

1 small bunch mixed
* parsley and coriander,*
* finely chopped*
75 g/3 oz spring onions,
* white part only, chopped*
175 g/6 oz chickpeas,
* soaked overnight*
1 small Spanish onion,
* finely chopped*
lemon juice

Crush the garlic with a pinch of salt then mix it with the ginger, pepper and saffron in a small bowl. Blend in half the butter then rub over the chicken. Put in a large dish, cover and leave in a cool place overnight.

Put the chicken and any juices left in the dish in a saucepan that will just fit the chicken. Add half of the herbs, the spring onions, the cinnamon stick and chickpeas and enough water to just cover. Heat to simmering point, then cook gently for about 1¼–1½ hours until tender, turning the chicken a couple of times.

Meanwhile, melt the remaining butter in a small pan, then add the Spanish onion and cook until softened, without allowing it to colour. Lift the chicken from the pan, draining the liquid from the cavity back into the pan, and keep the chicken warm.

Add the onion and most of the remaining herbs to the cooking liquor and simmer until the liquid is reduced to a sauce. Add lemon juice to taste. Discard the cinnamon.

Joint the chicken and pile the joints on a warm deep serving plate. Pour over the chunky sauce and sprinkle with the remaining parsley and coriander.

Chicken Tagine with Tomatoes

DJEJ MATISHA MESLA

Fragrant honey added at the end gives distinctive flavour and depending on the quality of the tomatoes, you may like to add some lemon juice just to lift the flavour.

SERVES 4

1 chicken, weighing about
   1.6 kg/3½ lb, jointed
1.5 kg/3¼ lb well-
   flavoured tomatoes,
   peeled and chopped
1 Spanish onion, grated
1 garlic clove, crushed
pinch of crushed saffron
   threads

2 tsp ground cinnamon
¼ tsp ground ginger
40 g/1½ oz unsalted butter
   or oil
salt and pepper
2 tbsp fragrant honey
toasted blanched almonds
   and sesame seeds, to
   garnish

Put all the ingredients except the honey and garnish, in a large, heavy flameproof casserole. Heat just to simmering point then cover and cook gently for about 1 hour until the chicken is extremely tender.

Remove the chicken and keep warm. Boil the cooking juices, stirring frequently, until well reduced and beginning to caramelize around the edges. Over a low heat stir in the honey then return the chicken to the casserole and turn to coat in the sauce. Serve with the almonds and sesame seeds sprinkled over.

Twice-cooked Chicken with Fragrant Sauce

DJEJ MAHAMMER

*The chicken in this Rabat version of a Moroccan dish, is first braised with plenty
of onion and aromatic spices, then browned in butter. The braising liquid is
reduced to make a sauce for serving with the chicken.*

SERVES 6

2 chickens, each weighing
about 1.4 kg/3 lb
2 Spanish onions, finely
chopped
2 garlic cloves, finely
chopped
pinch of saffron threads,
crushed

scant ½ tsp ground ginger
½ tsp freshly ground black
pepper
salt
300 ml/½ pt water
115 ml/6 fl oz olive oil
100 g/3½ oz unsalted
butter

Put the chicken in a large saucepan with the
remaining ingredients except the oil and butter.
Cover, bring just to simmering point, skim the scum
from the surface then simmer very gently for 1–1¼
hours, turning the chicken occasionally and adding a
little hot water, if necessary. Lift the chicken from
the pan, tilting so the liquid in the cavity flows out.

Heat the oil and butter in a large frying pan, add
the chicken and fry until golden. Meanwhile, boil
the liquid in the saucepan until thickened to a sauce.
Serve the sauce with the chicken.

Pigeon with Oranges

*Pigeon cotes are a common sight in rural and urban areas of North Africa. These
birds are small and tender, more like our farm-reared pigeons than wild ones.*

SERVES 6
3 tbsp olive oil
6 young pigeons
225 g/8 oz button onions,
    peeled
1 cinnamon stick
1 bay leaf
¾–1 tsp grated fresh
    ginger
large pinch saffron threads,
    toasted and crushed

850 ml/1½ pt chicken
    stock
salt and pepper
2 tbsp clear honey
2 oranges, peeled and
    thickly sliced
lightly toasted almond
    halves, to garnish

Heat the oil in a large, heavy, flameproof casserole,
add the pigeons in batches and cook until browned.
Using a slotted spoon, transfer to a dish. Stir the
onions into the casserole and sauté until golden. Stir
in the cinnamon, bay leaf, ginger, saffron, stock and
seasoning and bring to the boil. Return the pigeons
to the casserole with any juices that have collected in
the dish, cover and cook gently for about 1 hour,
depending on their age, turning the pigeons
occasionally, until they start to be tender.

Add the honey, cover again then cook for a further
30–45 minutes until the pigeons are very tender.
Using a slotted spoon, transfer the pigeons to a large
warmed serving plate, cover and keep warm.

Boil the cooking liquid until lightly thickened,
adding the orange slices towards the end. Discard
the cinnamon and bay leaf, if liked. Pour the liquid
over the pigeons and scatter over the almonds.

LEFT *Pigeon with Oranges*

Chicken Kdra with Almonds

—————— DJEJ BIL LOOZ ——————

*A kdra is a particular kind of tagine. Almonds become beautifully tender during
the long, slow simmering and lemon juice is added at the end to cut the richness.*

SERVES 4
1 chicken weighing about
    1.6 kg/3½ lb, jointed
1 Spanish onion, thinly
    sliced
115 g/4 oz blanched
    almonds
½ tsp ground cinnamon

pinch of crushed saffron
    threads
½ tsp ground ginger
50 g/2 oz unsalted butter
1 large bunch of parsley,
    finely chopped
squeeze of lemon juice
salt and pepper

Put all the ingredients, except the parsley and lemon
juice, into a saucepan. Just cover with water, bring to
simmering point then cover and cook gently for
about 1 hour until the chicken is very tender and
almost falling off the bones.

Transfer the chicken to a warm serving plate and
keep warm. Boil the liquid to reduce to a sauce,
adding the parsley, and lemon juice to taste just
before the end of cooking.

Chicken with Prunes, Honey and Cinnamon

—————— DJAL BIL BARGOUG WA ASSEL ——————

*In this Moroccan recipe the chicken is cooked with cinnamon, while the prunes
are cooked separately and made into a sauce with the cooking liquor.*

SERVES 4

2 tbsp olive oil

4 chicken portions

small piece of cinnamon
   stick

3 well-flavoured tomatoes,
   peeled and chopped

425 ml/15 fl oz chicken
   stock

salt and pepper

115 g/4 oz ready-to-eat
   prunes

1 tbsp clear honey

1 tbsp grated fresh ginger

50 g/2 oz raisins

pinch of saffron threads,
   crushed

150 ml/¼ pt water

toasted sesame seeds, to
   garnish

Heat the oil in a pan, brown the chicken, then add
the cinnamon, tomatoes, stock and seasoning. Bring
just to boiling point, then cover and simmer gently
for 45 minutes, removing the lid towards the end.

Meanwhile, cook the prunes with the honey,
ginger, raisins and saffron in the liquid for about 15
minutes until tender. Transfer the chicken to a warm
serving dish and keep warm.

Boil the cooking juices until reduced to 150 ml/5 fl
oz. Add to the prunes and heat together for a minute
or so. Pour over the chicken and garnish with
toasted sesame seeds.

Chicken Stuffed with Dried Fruit

*This Berber dish is a good example of the North African predilection for
combining meat and fruit. Stuff the neck cavity as well as the back cavity, which
must not be packed too tightly. Warm through left over stuffing and
serve with couscous.*

SERVES 4

5 tbsp olive oil

1 onion, chopped

25 g/1 oz pine nuts or
   almonds, chopped

225 g/8 oz mixed dried
   fruit – apricots, apples,
   pears, prunes, raisins,
   soaked, drained and
   chopped

salt and pepper

1.5 kg/3¼ lb chicken

RIGHT *Chicken with
Prunes, Honey and
Cinnamon*

Preheat the oven to 150–175°C/300–325°F/Gas 2–3.
Heat 2 tbsp oil in a pan, then cook the onion until
pale gold. Stir in the nuts and cook for 2–3 minutes,
then add the dried fruits and seasoning. Leave to
cool. Stuff the chicken with the dried-fruit mixture
and truss the bird. Brown the chicken in the
remaining oil in a large heavy flameproof casserole.
Sprinkle with salt and pepper and put the chicken on
one side. Cover the dish and cook in the oven for 1½
hours, turning the chicken every 30 minutes so it is
breast uppermost for the last 30 minutes.

Moroccan Pigeon (or Chicken) Pie

B'STILLA

B'stilla is one of the great dishes of North Africa. It is served hot-to-the-touch as a first course. To eat it, the thumb and first two fingers of the right hand are plunged through the crust into the steaming filling and the size of morsel required is pulled out.

In Morocco the crust is made of tissue-thin warka *but if you are not in Morocco, filo pastry is the most practical type to use, although it will not produce quite the same fine, crisp pie. Traditionally, the poultry portions are left whole but the pie is easier to eat if the bones are removed after cooking. This recipe, from Fez, is a fairly simple version.*

SERVES 8

2 young pigeons, or 1 medium chicken, jointed
2 Spanish onions, grated
½ tsp ground ginger
½ tsp crushed saffron threads
2½ tsp ground cinnamon
oil
salt and pepper
2 bunches of coriander, chopped

2 bunches of parsley, chopped
8 small eggs, beaten
10 sheets of filo pastry
115 g/4 oz blanched almonds, coarsely chopped and toasted
icing sugar (optional)
ground cinnamon and icing sugar for sprinkling

Put the poultry in a large saucepan with the onions, ginger, saffron, ½ tsp cinnamon, 3 tbsp oil, and seasoning. Add just a little water, so the birds are braised and not boiled. Cover and cook gently, turning the poultry occasionally until tender.

Remove the joints from the pan and leave until cool enough to handle. Discard the skin, and bone the joints, if liked. Add the coriander and parsley to the pan and boil until reduced to a thick, dryish sauce. Over a very low heat, stir in the eggs to scramble them. Remove from the heat.

Preheat the oven to 190°C/375°F/gas 5. Thoroughly oil a metal baking tin about 32 cm/13 in diameter and 5 cm/2 in deep. Lay a sheet of filo pastry in the tin, fitting it in to the shape of the tin and allowing any loose edges to fall over the sides. Brush with oil. Repeat with four more sheets, brushing with oil, so the tin is completely covered.

Cover with the pigeon or chicken pieces, then the egg mixture. Cover with a small sheet of pastry and scatter over the almonds. Sprinkle with 2 tsp cinnamon, and a little icing sugar, if liked. Fold overhanging edges of pastry over the almonds then cover with the remaining pastry, brushing each sheet with oil. Tuck the edges inside the tin and under the pie. Bake for about 45 minutes until crisp and golden. Sieve icing sugar over the top and make a lattice with ground cinnamon. Serve hot.

5
Meats

Lamb is far and away the most popular meat in North Africa; Islam forbids pork, and goats are used for milk rather than meat. Whole baby lamb are sometimes roasted, as for the Berber *mechoui,* traditionally prepared for festivals and ceremonies in the desert but now also cooked in towns and cities. Also, cubes of lamb, often first marinated in *Chermoula,* are threaded on skewers and grilled over charcoal; but most common of all are the succulent slow-cooked lamb dishes, braised very gently in fragrant *tagines* until the meat becomes so tender it can be broken apart with bread.

Lamb Tagine with Fennel

——— TAGINE EL LAHM BESBAS ———

*The flavours of fennel, lemon and lamb make a delicious combination. In
Morocco wild fennel is sometimes used, but the Florence fennel that we have is
just as effective in this dish.*

SERVES 4–6

1.1 kg/2½ lb lean shoulder
of lamb, cut into 3 cm/
1½ in cubes
1 onion, grated
2 garlic cloves, crushed
2 tbsp chopped coriander
pinch of crushed saffron
threads
¾ tsp ground ginger
½ tsp freshly ground black
pepper

225 ml/8 fl oz water
3 fennel bulbs, thickly
sliced
2 tbsp lemon juice
salt
1 Preserved Lemon in salt
(see page 125), quartered,
flesh discarded if liked,
and rinsed
75 g/3 oz Kalamata olives

Mix the lamb, onion, garlic, coriander and spices
together in a heavy, flameproof casserole. Pour over
the water, bring just to simmering point then cover
and cook gently for about 1¼ hours until the lamb is
almost tender.

Add the fennel, lemon juice and salt, cover and
cook for a further 20 minutes or so, until the lamb
and fennel are tender. Transfer the lamb and fennel
to a warm serving dish. Scatter over the Preserved
Lemon and olives, cover and keep warm.

If necessary, boil the cooking juices to reduce and
thicken. Pour over the lamb and fennel and serve.

Lamb Tagine with Chestnuts and Chickpeas

——— MARQUIT QUASTAL ———

*This wonderfully fragrant stew is often made with dried chestnuts, because they
are more practical in Tunisia, but the flavour is even better when fresh chestnuts
are used.*

SERVES 4

3 tbsp olive oil
1 onion, chopped
2 celery sticks, chopped
2 garlic cloves, crushed
115 g/4 oz chickpeas,
soaked overnight, then
drained

450 g/1 lb lean lamb,
cubed
1 tsp ground cinnamon
pepper
450 g/1 lb chestnuts,
peeled
2 tbsp raisins
salt

Heat the oil in a heavy flameproof casserole then
add the onion, celery and garlic and cook until
softened. Stir in the lamb and brown evenly, then
add the chickpeas. Cover with water and bring to
the boil, remove the scum from the surface with a
slotted spoon. Add the cinnamon and a generous
grinding of black pepper, but no salt, cover and cook
gently for 1¼–1½ hours until the lamb and
chickpeas are almost tender.

Add the chestnuts, raisins and salt to the casserole
and cook for a further 15–20 minutes until all the
ingredients are tender.

RIGHT *Lamb Tagine with
Fennel*

Moroccan Lamb with Apricots

―――――― SIKBADJ ――――――

Tunisian apricots are darker, firmer and sharper tasting than those commonly available to us. The nearest equivalents can usually be found in healthfood shops or local food markets.
Aubergines are sometimes included in this recipe, and saffron-flavoured rice makes a good accompaniment.

SERVES 4

675 g/1½ lb lean lamb, cubed
2 garlic cloves, crushed
5 tbsp orange juice
4 tbsp olive oil
1 tbsp chopped fresh coriander
1 tbsp chopped fresh mint
1 tsp ground cumin
pinch of freshly grated nutmeg

1 onion, thinly sliced
150 g/5 oz dried apricots, soaked overnight just covered by water
50 g/2 oz pitted dried dates, coarsely chopped
500 ml/17 fl oz stock
salt and pepper
2 tbsp sesame seeds, to garnish

In a large non-metallic dish, mix the lamb with the garlic, orange juice, 2 tbsp olive oil, the herbs and spices. Cover and leave overnight in the refrigerator, stirring occasionally.

Heat the remaining oil in a flameproof casserole, then add the onion and cook gently, for 5 minutes. Remove and reserve.

Drain the lamb, reserving the marinade. Quickly brown the lamb in the casserole then add the reserved marinade, the apricots and soaking liquid, dates, stock, onion and seasoning. Bring just to the boil, then cover and cook gently for about 1 hour until the lamb is very tender. Uncover towards the end of the cooking to allow some of the liquid to evaporate and thicken the sauce. Serve sprinkled with sesame seeds.

Lamb Tagine with Prunes

—————— TAGINE BARROGOG BIS BASELA ——————

When the Andalusian Moors left Spain after the reconquest, and settled in Fez and Tetouan, the cooking of northern Morocco experienced a renaissance. This recipe is typical of the festive meat and fruit dishes originating from that time. The sweetness of the prunes and honey is counterbalanced by the spices and generous seasoning with black pepper.

SERVES 6-8

3 tbsp olive oil
1 large onion, grated
2 garlic cloves, chopped
900 g/2 lb lean lamb, cut
   into large pieces
small bunch of parsley,
   finely chopped
2 tsp freshly ground black
   pepper
1 tsp ground ginger
½ tsp crushed saffron
   threads

400 g/14 oz prunes, just
   covered by water and
   soaked overnight
2 tsp ground cinnamon
salt
1–3 tbsp orange-flower
   water, to taste
about 2 tbsp clear honey, to
   taste
toasted sesame seeds and
   pine nuts or chopped
   almonds, to garnish

Stir the oil, onion, garlic, lamb, parsley, pepper and spices together in a heavy, flameproof casserole. Add the prune soaking liquid and enough water to just cover. Cover the casserole and cook gently for about 1 hour until the lamb is almost tender.

Add the prunes, cinnamon and salt, cover again and cook for a further 30 minutes. Stir in orange-flower water and honey to taste and cook for a few more minutes. Serve garnished with toasted sesame seeds and pine nuts or almonds.

Saffron-baked Lamb

—————— AGNEAU AU FOUR ——————

A rich and subtle Tunisian dish.

SERVES 6

1.1 kg/2½ lb waxy
   potatoes, peeled
salt and pepper
pinch of saffron threads

1.4 kg/3 lb leg of lamb, in
   steaks, or chopped
100 ml/3½ fl oz olive oil
juice of 1 lemon

Quarter the potatoes lengthways, put into a bowl with the saffron and just cover with salted water. Leave for 30 minutes.

Preheat the oven to 180°C/350°F/gas 4. Drain the potatoes and reserve 300 ml/½ pt of the soaking liquid. Layer the potatoes and lamb in a baking dish, pouring over the oil and lemon juice, and seasoning as you go. Pour over the reserved saffron liquid, cover and bake for 1½ hours until the lamb is tender.

LEFT *Saffron-baked lamb*

Lamb braised with Herbs

—————— T'DLLA ——————

In the authentic way of the desert, the lamb is braised by laying hot coals on the top of the tagine slaoui. *When the dish is eaten, bread is rubbed lightly over the lamb then dipped in the sauce (which would be much richer in butter or* smen *than in this version). A piece of meat is then removed from the joint with the fingers, or using a small piece of bread if the meat is very hot.*

SERVES 5–6

1 Spanish onion, finely
   chopped
2 garlic cloves, finely
   chopped
½ tsp ground cinnamon
½ tsp cumin
½ tsp ginger
¼ tsp crushed toasted
   saffron threads
pinch of cayenne pepper

salt
5 tbsp olive oil
5 tbsp water
1 shoulder of lamb, about
   1.75 g/4 lb
75 g/3 oz butter, softened,
   plus more for browning,
   if liked
chopped coriander, to serve
   (if liked)

Preheat the oven to 190°C/375°F/gas 5. Mix together the onion, garlic, spices, salt, oil and water. Put half the mixture in the bottom of a heavy flameproof casserole or baking tin, large enough to hold the lamb. Rub the remaining mixture into the lamb and put in the casserole or dish. Spread over the butter. Cook over a high heat until the lamb is brown.

Add just enough water to come halfway up the joint and heat until it comes to the boil. Cover with a lid or foil and cook in the oven for about 2 hours until the lamb is so tender it pulls easily from the bone. If liked, then remove the lid, baste with extra butter and brown lamb under a hot grill until crisp and golden. Stir some chopped coriander into the cooking juices, before serving.

Lamb with Coriander Marinade

LABAN IMMO

When translated, the name of this Arab dish means "his mother's milk", because the young lamb is marinated in ewe's milk yogurt, before cooking.

SERVES 4

2 garlic cloves
salt
1 dried red chilli, seeded
  and chopped
1.25 cm/½ in piece fresh
  ginger, chopped
1½ tbsp coriander
1 tbsp coriander seeds,
  crushed

1½ tsp ground coriander
1 tsp ground cumin
1 tsp ground turmeric
300 ml/½ pt Greek
  sheep's milk yogurt
1 tbsp lemon juice
600 g/1¼ lb lean lamb,
  cubed
sprigs of coriander, to
  garnish

Crush the garlic with a pinch of salt in a pestle and mortar, or with the end of a rolling pin in a bowl. Add the chilli, ginger and coriander and work to a paste. Mix in the ground spices then stir in the yogurt and lemon juice.

Put the lamb in a non-metallic bowl, pour over the yogurt mixture, stir to mix then cover and leave in a cool place for 2–8 hours.

Preheat the grill or barbecue. Thread the lamb onto skewers and grill or barbecue, turning occasionally, until the meat is brown on the outside and pink in the centre. Serve garnished with coriander sprigs.

Lamb Tagine with Quinces

SAFARDJALIYA

Firm apples or pears can be substituted, but they do not have the same luscious fragrance.

SERVES 6–8

2 tbsp oil
1 large onion, chopped
900 g/2 lb lean lamb,
  cubed
1 tsp ground cinnamon
½ tsp ground ginger
½ tsp saffron threads,
  crushed

2 large, well-flavoured
  tomatoes, peeled and
  chopped
675 g/1½ lb quinces
juice of ½ lemon
1 tbsp clear honey
salt and pepper

Heat the oil in a heavy flameproof casserole then add the onion and cook until tender. Add the meat, cook until evenly browned then stir in the spices for about 1 minute. Add the tomatoes and enough water to just cover. Cover the casserole and cook gently for about 1 hour until the lamb is tender.

Meanwhile, scrub the quinces. Cut into eighths, quarters or halves depending on size. Remove the cores and any blemishes, but not the peel as it adds flavour and a gelatinous quality to the casserole.

Add the quinces, lemon, honey and seasoning and cook for a further 15–30 minutes until the quinces are tender; take care that they do not fall apart.

RIGHT *Lamb with Coriander Marinade*

Lamb with Chickpeas and Apricots

MISHMISHEYA

Tunisians usually add sugar to this dish, but if the apricots are ripe and well-flavoured you will probably find it sweet enough without adding any (although you might like to try sweetening it for an authentic taste).

SERVES 4–6

3 tbsp olive oil
1 Spanish onion, chopped
675 g/1½ lb lean lamb, cubed
175 g/6 oz chickpeas, soaked overnight and drained
2–2½ tsp ground cinnamon
550 g/1¼ lb well-flavoured ripe fresh apricots, halved and pitted
salt and pepper

Heat the oil in a large pan, then add the onion and fry until soft and golden. Stir in the meat, cook until evenly browned then add the chickpeas and enough water to cover. Bring just to the boil, skim the scum from the surface, then add the cinnamon. Simmer for about 1 hour until the lamb and chickpeas are almost tender. Add the apricots and seasoning and cook for about 20 minutes until all the chickpeas are cooked and the meat is very tender.

Spicy Sausages

MERGUEZ

Merguez make a tasty alternative to ordinary "bangers", although some people may find them too spicy to eat for breakfast! They should be well flavoured, so add more spices if necessary (to test the flavour, break off a small piece and fry to cook before tasting).

SERVES 4

350 g/12 oz beef, cubed
150 g/5 oz beef fat, cubed
1 tsp paprika
1 tsp mixed ground cinnamon and cloves, crumbled dried thyme and cayenne
salt and pepper
2–4 tbsp chilled water
sausage casings
1–2 garlic cloves, coarsely chopped

Pass the beef, fat and garlic through a hand mincer, then mix thoroughly with spices and seasonings; or mix the beef, fat, garlic, spices and seasonings in a food processor. Add a little water to moisten.

Fill the casing with the meat mixture, tying into 5 cm/2 in sausages. Hang in an airy, warmish, dry place to dry for 24 hours.

Fry, grill or boil the sausages and eat hot or cold.

Honeyed Lamb

MROUZIA

In the days when refrigeration and freezing were uncommon, this rich, sweet Moroccan tagine was prepared after the celebration of the Aid el Kebir, the Feast of the Slaughter of the Lamb in order to preserve the meat. I have reduced the amount of honey in the recipe, but it is still quite a sweet dish, so I balance the flavour with lemon juice. Make the tagine 24 hours in advance (it will actually keep much longer) then reheat it gently when required. Because of its sweetness it is never served on its own but in combination with lighter dishes.

SERVES 6

115 g/4 oz butter
pinch of saffron threads
1 tsp freshly ground black pepper
1 tsp ground cinnamon
2 tsp Ras el hanout (see page 118)
salt

1.4 kg/3 lb middle neck of lamb, with bone
225 g/8 oz raisins
3 onions, finely chopped
175 g/6 oz blanched almonds
150 ml/¼ pt water
175 g/6 oz clear honey
lemon juice

In a small bowl, crush the saffron with the remaining spices and a pinch of salt. Rub most of the mixture into the lamb and mix the remainder with the raisins.

Put the lamb and remaining ingredients, except the raisins, honey and lemon juice, in a pan, bring to the boil then cover and cook gently, stirring occasionally, for about 1–1¼ hours until the meat is almost tender; add more water if necessary to prevent the meat catching on the pan.

Stir in the raisins, honey and a good squeeze of lemon juice and cook, uncovered, for a further 30 minutes until almost all the liquid has evaporated, leaving a rich, thick sauce.

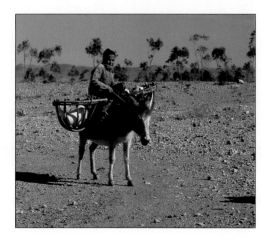

LEFT *Pack donkey, Hassi-Berkane, Morocco*

Spiced Lamb topped with Tomatoes

--------- M'FKOUL ---------

*Cooked slowly under a blanket of well-browned onions, lamb shanks become
wonderfully succulent and tender.*

SERVES 6

1½ tsp ground cinnamon
¼ tsp ground cumin
¼ tsp ginger
1 small bunch of parsley,
  chopped
1 small bunch of coriander,
  chopped
6 lamb shanks each
  weighing about 225 g/
  8 oz and 5 cm/2 in thick

3 tbsp olive oil
1½ Spanish onions, finely
  chopped
salt and pepper
1½ tbsp tomato purée
3 large, ripe well-flavoured
  tomatoes, peeled, seeded
  and halved
caster sugar

Mix together the cinnamon, cumin, ginger, parsley
and coriander in a small bowl. Spread over the lamb
and leave in a cool place for 3–4 hours.

Heat 2½ tbs oil in a heavy flameproof casserole,
add the onion, sprinkle with salt and cook very
gently, stirring occasionally, until browned and
caramelized. Remove from the casserole. Preheat the
oven to 170°C/325°F/gas 3.

Brown the lamb in the casserole, adding more oil
as necessary. Add any remaining spice and herb
mixture and seasoning then cover the lamb with
the onions. Blend a little water with the tomato
purée in a jug, then pour over the onions. Add
sufficient water to almost cover, bring to just on
simmering point then cover tightly and cook in the
oven for about 1 hour 40 minutes until the lamb
is tender.

Put a tomato half, cut side down, on each lamb
shank. Check the seasoning and spicing of the
cooking liquid, then baste the tomatoes. Sprinkle
with caster sugar, cover and return to the oven for
20 minutes.

ABOVE *Colourful spices and baskets shop in Essaouira, Morocco*

6
Vegetables

The inland areas of North Africa are too hot for cultivating vegetables, but in the fertile belt nearer the coast, however, vegetables thrive. As well as being served as side dishes with cooked meats, they are frequently combined with meat, poultry, grains or other vegetables in stews and served over mounds of *couscous*. North African vegetable dishes are often so good they can be served as a course in their own right, and are perfect for vegetarians.

Spiced Potato Cakes

These tasty fried potato cakes come from Algeria. The spicy mashed potato mixture is also good served simply as it is.

SERVES 4–6

900 g/2 lb mashed potato
1 tbsp paprika pepper
2 tsp ground cumin
good pinch of cayenne
 pepper
1 bunch of coriander,
 chopped
3 eggs
salt and pepper
oil for frying

In a large bowl, mix the potato with the spices, coriander, eggs and seasoning. With floured hands, form the mixture into round flat cakes. Cover and chill for 30 minutes.

Heat a shallow layer of oil in a frying pan, add the cakes in batches and fry until crisp and brown on both sides. Transfer to paper towels to drain. Serve hot.

Spiced Parsnips

MZOURA I

This version of Tunisian Mzoura is sweet and spicy, and made as hot as you like with Harissa. I have also tasted it made, more traditionally, with carrots.

SERVES 4–6

900 g/2 lb small parsnips,
 sliced
3 tbsp olive oil
1 small onion, finely
 chopped
1 garlic clove, finely
 chopped
1 tsp Harissa (see
 page 120)
1 tsp ground cumin
1 tsp ground coriander
1 tsp clear honey
150 ml/¼ pt vegetable
 stock
salt and pepper
chopped coriander, to
 garnish

Cook the parsnips in a saucepan of boiling water for about 7 minutes, then drain. Meanwhile, heat the oil in a frying pan, then add the onion and garlic and cook gently until softened. Stir in the *Harissa* and spices, then add the honey, stock, parsnips and seasoning. Cook for 7–10 minutes, until the parsnips are tender and the liquid reduced to a sauce. Serve hot or cold sprinkled with coriander.

RIGHT Above *Spiced Parsnips* Below *Spiced Potato Cakes*

Cracked Barley and Broad Bean Couscous

────── CHEESHA SIKUK ──────

*Cracked barley, which is available from healthfood shops, makes a delicious,
nutty-flavoured couscous. This recipe is from Morocco.*

SERVES 4

450 g/1 lb cracked barley
75 g/3 oz butter, diced
150 g/5 oz shelled small
   broad beans
2 plump spring onions,
   sliced
salt and pepper

Rinse the barley under running cold water then leave
to drain for 3 minutes. Butter the top container of a
couscousier or a metal colander or steamer lined
with muslin.

Squeeze the barley to expel excess water and put
into the top part of the *couscousier,* rubbing the grains
to separate them. Cover the container with muslin,
then a lid, and put over the bottom part of a boiling
couscousier. Steam for 20 minutes.

Tip the barley into a large roasting tin and break
up lumps with a fork. Add 15 g/½ oz butter and very
slowly pour in 450 ml/¾ pt water so the grains do
not become soggy, forking through and stirring the
barley to keep the grains separate. Leave to dry for
10 minutes before re-covering and placing back on
the bottom part of the *couscousier.* Steam for a further
20 minutes.

Tip the barley into the roasting tin again, break up
any lumps and leave for 15 minutes. Meanwhile,
cook the beans and spring onions in a small amount
of boiling salted water until tender. Drain and stir
into the barley with the remaining butter.

ABOVE *Low-level, flat-roofed houses, typical of North African dwellings*

Aromatic Chickpea Tagine

--------- TAGINE BIL HUMMUS ---------

In Morocco, chickpeas are sometimes peeled to make a more "refined" dish. The chickpeas are left in sunlight to soak, then drained and rubbed against the sides of a reed basket to remove their skins.

SERVES 4–6

900 g/2 lb chickpeas, soaked overnight and drained
4 tbsp olive oil
pinch of saffron threads, crushed
¼ tsp paprika
¼ tsp ground cumin
¼ tsp ginger
¼ tsp cinnamon

3 large well-flavoured tomatoes, peeled, seeded and chopped
1 Spanish onion, coarsely grated
4 sprigs of coriander, chopped
6 sprigs of parsley, chopped
salt, black pepper and chilli pepper

Cook the chickpeas in boiling water until tender. Drain, and peel if liked.

Heat the oil in a large saucepan, stir in the saffron and other spices and cook until fragrant, then add the tomatoes, onion, coriander, parsley, chickpeas and seasoning. Cover and heat through gently for about 15 minutes, stirring occasionally.

Onion Tagine

--------- MEZGALDI ---------

Traditionally, the tagine *is covered with a concave lid, and glowing coals are put into the lid so the onions cook from above as well as below. In modern homes with cookers, the oven and grill are used.*

SERVES 4–6

1 tsp ground ginger
1 tsp crushed black peppercorns
4 tbsp ground cinnamon
2 tbsp caster sugar
¼ tsp crushed saffron threads

salt
900 g/2 lb Spanish onions, sliced
115 ml/4 fl oz olive oil
2 celery stalks

In a small bowl, mix together the ginger, black peppercorns, half the cinnamon and sugar, the saffron and salt. Place the onion slices and spice mixture in layers in a non-metallic bowl. Pour over the oil and leave for 2 hours.

Arrange the celery crosswise in a *tagine* or heavy flameproof casserole. Add the onions and spice. In a small bowl, mix together the remaining sugar and cinnamon, then sprinkle over the onions. Cover and cook in an oven preheated to 170°C/325°F/gas 3 for 40–50 minutes until the onions are meltingly tender. Brown under a hot grill.

Couscous with Dried Apricots and Almonds

This quick, light, simple modern couscous recipe was developed to suit the type of couscous now most widely available (see page 11). You can stir in butter or oil in the traditional way, or leave it out.

SERVES 8

350 g/12 oz pre-cooked couscous (see page 11)
75 g/3 oz ready-to-eat dried apricots, sliced into strips
salt and pepper
50 g/3 oz blanched almonds, lightly toasted
chopped fresh coriander, to serve
unsalted butter or olive oil, to serve, if liked

Put the *couscous* in a bowl and pour over 570 ml/1 pt water. Leave for about 30 minutes or until most of the water has been absorbed; stir frequently with a fork to keep the grains separate. Stir the apricots and seasoning into the *couscous* then tip into a *couscousier* or steamer or metal colander lined with muslin. Place over a saucepan of boiling water, cover tightly with foil and steam for about 20 minutes until hot. Stir in the almonds, coriander and butter or oil, if using.

Mixeᴅ Vegetable Tagine

The original recipe I was given for this tagine *contained 75 g/3 oz raisins, but I prefer the dish without them. You may like to add them when you make it – it's a matter of taste. Serve the* tagine *over couscous or rice.*

SERVES 4

115 g/4 oz chickpeas,
  soaked overnight, then
  drained chopped
3 tbsp olive oil
4 small carrots, sliced
2 onions, chopped
3 garlic cloves, chopped
1 green pepper, sliced
2 courgettes, thickly sliced
1 tsp ground coriander

1 tsp ground cumin
3 tomatoes, chopped
570 ml/1 pt stock
salt and pepper
juice of 1 lemon
2 tbsp chopped fresh
  parsley, to garnish
4 spring onions, white part
  only, finely chopped, to
  garnish

Cook the chickpeas in plenty of boiling water until tender; the time will depend on the age and variety of the chickpeas.

Meanwhile, heat the oil in a pan, add the carrot and fry until browned. Remove and reserve. Add the onion and garlic to the pan and cook gently until soft and golden. Add the pepper and courgettes and cook until softened. Stir in the spices and cook until fragrant, then add the tomatoes, carrots, stock and seasoning. Bring to the boil.

Drain the chickpeas, add to the vegetable mixture, cover and simmer for about 30 minutes until all the vegetables are tender. Stir in the lemon juice and sprinkle over the parsley and spring onions.

Okra and Tomato Tagine

──────── MARAK MATISHA BIL MELOKHIAS ────────

Be sure to choose small okra pods. In Tetuan, the okra pods are threaded on string, so they can be lifted out when the tagine is stirred. Served as a main course or with grilled or roast meats and poultry.

SERVES 4

450 g/1 lb fresh okra
3 tbsp olive oil
1 large onion, finely
   chopped
2 garlic cloves, finely
   chopped
675 g/1½ lb well-
   flavoured tomatoes,
   peeled, seeded and
   chopped

pinch of paprika pepper
4 tbsp chopped fresh
   parsley
salt and pepper

Trim the stalk off the okra without cutting the pod. Heat the oil in a pan and fry the okra until lightly browned. Remove with a slotted spoon.

Add the onion and garlic to the pan and fry until soft but not browned. Stir in the paprika, stirring for 30 seconds, then add the tomatoes. Bring to the boil and simmer for 10 minutes. Add the okra, half the parsley, plenty of pepper and a little salt. Simmer, occasionally stirring, for about 30 minutes.

If the sauce is not well-reduced, transfer the okra to a warm dish and keep warm. Boil the sauce until thickened. Pour over the okra. Serve warm or cold, sprinkled with the remaining parsley.

Swiss Chard Tagine

──────── MARAK SILK ────────

There may appear to be too little liquid to cook the rice but the vegetables, especially the chard, give out a lot of moisture, too. The lid must fit really well so that no steam can escape (seal it with foil to be sure).

SERVES 4–6

900 g/2 lb Swiss chard
1 garlic clove, finely
   chopped
3 tbsp oil
1 tsp paprika

1 largish onion, finely
   chopped
40 g/1½ oz long grain rice
4 tbsp chopped fresh
   coriander
4 tbsp water
salt and pepper

Separate the leaf part from the thick ribs of the chard. Shred the leaves coarsely and slice the stalks into 1.25 cm/½ in wide strips.

Warm the oil in a heavy flameproof casserole, add the chard stalks and the garlic, cover and cook gently for 10–15 minutes, stirring occasionally. Stir in the paprika, stirring for 30–60 seconds, then the onion, chard leaves, rice, coriander, water and seasoning. Cover with a very tight-fitting lid and cook, stirring occasionally, for about 30 minutes until the rice is tender; if necessary add some more water.

RIGHT *Okra and Tomato Tagine*

Spiced Glazed Carrots with Dill

————— MZOURA 2 —————

Dill, ginger and orange produce this distinctive version of Mzoura. Shake the pan towards the end of cooking to prevent the carrots from sticking.

SERVES 4

450 g/1 lb carrots, cut into
  thin sticks
25 g/1 oz butter
1 tbsp sugar

1.25 cm/½ in piece of fresh
  ginger, shredded
thickly grated rind of 1
  orange
salt and pepper
few sprigs of dill, chopped

Put the carrots, butter, sugar, ginger, orange rind and seasoning in a pan and just cover with water. Bring to the boil then simmer for about 12 minutes until the carrots are tender and the liquid has evaporated.

7

Desserts, Pastries and Breads

Sweet cakes and pastries are normally eaten with glasses of tea at any time of day, and are offered to guests and served by the trayful at special occasions such as festivals and family celebrations.

Bread is sacred in North Africa: according to a Moroccan story, a woman who defiled a loaf was imprisoned in the moon. Bread has to be treated with respect, and if a piece is seen lying on the ground it must be picked up, kissed and put somewhere so that it will not become dirty.

At dinner, it is customary for only one person to cut the flat, round loaves into wedges and distribute them around the table.

Almond Biscuits

―――――― GHORIBA BIL LOZ ――――――

These rich, cracked almond biscuits are a popular Arab sweetmeat. They are delicious served with coffee.

MAKES ABOUT 30

2 small eggs
200 g/7 oz icing sugar,
　plus extra for coating
400 g/14 oz ground
　almonds

grated rind of ½ lemon
2 tsp baking powder
orange-flower or rose
　water, to taste

Preheat the oven to 180°C/350°F/gas 4. Oil a baking sheet. In a mixing bowl, beat 1 whole egg, 1 egg yolk and the sugar thoroughly together, then mix in the ground almonds, lemon rind, baking powder and orange-flower or rose water to taste. Knead well with your hands to release the oil from the almonds, and add some of the remaining egg white if necessary to make a soft, workable paste.

Using oiled hands, roll walnut-sized pieces of almond mixture into egg-shaped balls.

Cover a plate with icing sugar and flatten the balls on the icing sugar. Place, spaced quite well apart, on the baking sheet and bake for about 15 minutes until golden.

LEFT *Almond Biscuits*

Honeyed Almond Paste

―――――― AMALOU ――――――

This is a famous dish from the Souss region in southwest Morocco. Traditionally, it is made with highly flavoured oil produced by pressing the nuts from argan trees – these are unique to the region and have a famed attraction for goats, who literally climb up into the branches to get at the acid, pungent-flavoured nuts. Amalou is served with hot baked or fried bread or used as a filling for pancakes. Walnut oil makes a substitute for argan oil.

1 tbsp vegetable oil
225 g/8 oz blanched
　almonds

115 g/4 fl oz walnut oil
salt
4 tbsp thick honey

Heat a little vegetable oil in a pan, then add the almonds and brown. Drain on paper towels then process them in a blender with the walnut oil and salt until smooth and creamy. Add the honey and process briefly until well blended. Pour into a jar, cover and keep in the refrigerator. The paste should then keep for at least two months.

Fried Yeast Pastries

RGHAIF

The dough for these pastries is made in the same way as the dough for
croissants or Danish pastries (but without the butter), rolled and folded to make
it puffy and flaky.

SERVES 4

450 g/1 lb plain flour
1 tbsp instant dried yeast
1 egg, beaten

about 300 ml/½ pt water
oil for medium-deep frying
butter and honey, to serve

Stir together the flour and yeast in a mixing bowl, then slowly pour in enough water, stirring and then beating, to give a smooth, sticky, soft dough. Knead the dough thoroughly for about 20 minutes until it becomes firm and very elastic.

With oiled hands, divide the dough into 16–20 balls about the size of a prune. On an oiled surface and using oiled palms and fingers, pat and stretch each ball to a paper-thin rectangle about 25 x 22.5 cm/ 10 x 9 in; avoid tearing the dough and try to keep it evenly thin. Fold in the ends to meet at the centre. Turn the dough halfway round, then repeat the folding. Pat out again to a rectangle about 15 x 10 cm/ 4 x 6 in.

Heat a 1.25 cm/½ in depth of oil in a frying pan. Slip in one *rghaif* and fry until it puffs up and becomes crisp and golden underneath, spooning over a little hot oil as it cooks. Turn the *rghaif* over and fry for about 1 minute. Serve hot with butter and honey.

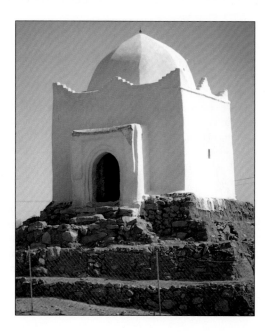

RIGHT *Mosabite tomb in Taggit, Algeria*

Walnut and Almond Sweets

———— FUSTUKH MAHCHI ————

Walnuts sandwiched together with a rosewater flavoured almond mixture make
a delicious way to end a meal Tunisian-style.

MAKES 12

115 g/4 oz ground almonds
1 tsp rose water
1 egg yolk
24 walnut halves

175 g/6 oz sugar, plus
   extra for coating
150 ml/¼ pt water
1 tbsp lemon juice

Mix the ground almonds with the rose water, then add enough egg yolk to bind the ingredients together. Use the almond mixture to sandwich together the walnut halves.

Gently heat the sugar in the water and lemon juice, stirring until the sugar has dissolved. Raise the heat and boil until the syrup has reduced by half.

Using a spoon and fork, lower the walnuts into the syrup and turn over. Lift out and roll in sugar to coat evenly. Leave to dry overnight.

Sweet Almond and Seed Powder

———— SELLOU ————

It is traditional to serve this at special celebrations, for guests to take a spoonful
or two as they are eating other sweets.

50 g/2 oz sesame seeds
50 g/2 oz chopped
   almonds
1 tbsp oil
½–1 tbsp anise seeds
225 g/8 oz plain flour

115 g/4 oz butter, chopped
50 g/2 oz sugar
¼–½ tsp icing sugar
whole or slivered almonds
   and icing sugar, to
   decorate

Scatter the sesame seeds in a grill pan, toast under the grill until golden and tip into a blender.

Mix the almonds with the oil in a grill pan and toast under the grill, stirring occasionally, until browned then add to the blender with the anise seeds and process until smooth.

Cook the flour in a large, heavy frying pan over a moderate heat, stirring constantly, until it has become golden brown. Remove from the heat. Melt the butter in a saucepan, stir in the flour and cook, stirring, until thick and caramel coloured, but do not allow to burn. Remove from the heat and stir the seed and nut mixture, the sugars and cinnamon into the butter. Allow to cool. Serve decorated with almonds and lines of icing sugar.

RIGHT *Walnut and Almond Sweets*

Gazelle's Horns

———— KAAB EL GHZAL ————

These popular curved, horn-shaped pastries, called tcharak *in Algeria, are often known abroad by their French name,* cornes de gazelles *and variations of them can be found in all the North African cuisines. If you prefer a more delicate orange-flower water flavour in the pastry, use part water and part orange-flower water to mix the dough.*

MAKES ABOUT 16

FOR THE FILLING:
200 g/7 oz blanched
  almonds, ground
100 g/3½ oz caster sugar
½ tsp ground cinnamon
about 2 tbsp orange-flower
  water

FOR THE PASTRY:
200 g/7 oz plain flour
pinch of salt
2 tbsp sunflower oil
150–175 ml/5–6 fl oz
  orange-flower water
icing sugar, for dusting

Mix the filling ingredients together and knead to a stiff paste; it will seem dry at first but will loosen up and stick together as the warmth of your hands releases the oil from the almonds. Set aside.

Preheat the oven to 189°C/350°F/gas 4. Oil a baking sheet. To make the pastry, sift the flour and salt in a mixing bowl and mix together with the oil. Stir in just enough orange-flower water to bring it together as a soft dough. Knead well until smooth and elastic.

On a lightly floured surface, roll out the dough very thinly and cut into 7.5 cm/3 in wide strips. Roll pieces of filling about the size of a walnut into thin sausage shapes about 7.5 cm/3 in long and with tapering ends. Place lengthways along the edge of the strips of dough, about 3 cm/1¼ in apart.

Dampen the pastry edges with water and fold over the pastry to cover the filling. Seal the edges. Cut around the humps of filling with a pastry or pasta cutter, or the point of a sharp knife and press the cut edges together to seal.

Carefully curve the pastries into horn or crescent shapes and put on the baking sheet. Bake for 20–25 minutes until lightly coloured. Leave to cool on a wire rack then dust with icing sugar.

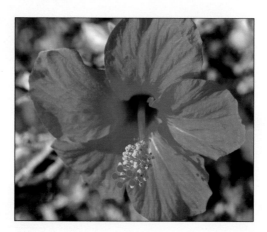

RIGHT *Hibiscus flowering in Carthage, Tunisia*

Peach Salad

The ancient Persians brought peaches to North Africa, as well as melons and pomegranates. I like to eat this light, delicately-perfumed fruit salad on its own, but it can be served with crème fraîche, cream, thick yogurt or ice cream.

SERVES 4

4 large ripe peaches, peeled if liked, and sliced
about 3 tbsp sugar

2–4 tsp rose or orange-flower water
mint leaves, to decorate, if liked

Put the peach slices in a shallow serving dish, sprinkle over the sugar and rose or orange-flower water and mix together gently. Cover and chill for 2 hours. Just before serving, scatter over a few mint leaves, if liked.

Honeycomb Yeast Pancakes

——— BEGHRIR ———

Like English crumpets, Beghrir are cooked on one side and bubbles burst on the surface to give a honeycomb effect. Butter and honey are, therefore, absorbed right into the pancakes. In Algeria, Beghrir are sometimes made from semolina.

SERVES 4–6

450 g/1 lb plain flour
1 tbsp instant dried yeast
1 egg, beaten
about 350 ml/12 fl oz water, or mixed water and milk

melted butter, and warm honey flavoured with orange-flower water, to serve

Stir together the flour and yeast in a mixing bowl. Add the egg, then slowly pour in the water or milk and water, stirring and then beating, to give a smooth batter, the consistency of thick cream. Set aside for about 1 hour.

Oil a griddle or heavy frying pan and heat over a medium heat. Pour about 3 tbsp of batter into the pan, rotating the pan so the batter flows evenly over the surface. Cook until bubbles appear and burst on the surface and the underside is light golden brown. Serve immediately or transfer to a large plate and keep warm while frying the remaining batter.

Arrange the pancakes in an overlapping circle around the plate, rather than stacking them as this makes them tough. Serve warm with melted butter, and warm honey flavoured with orange-flower water, trickled over.

LEFT *Peach Salad*

Cornflour Pudding

MUHALLABEYA

*Muhallabeya travelled to North Africa from the Middle East. It has a soothing,
silky-light, not-quite-set texture. Instead of the almond and pistachio decoration,
almonds can be fried until brown and crisp, then crushed and mixed with a little
cinnamon and sugar.*

SERVES 4–6

5 tbsp cornflour
about 3–5 tbsp sugar to
 taste
700 ml/1¼ pt creamy milk

2 tbsp orange-flower water
½ tsp grated lemon zest, if
 liked
50 g/2 oz mixed blanched
 almonds and pistachios

In a jug, blend the cornflour and sugar to a paste
with a little of the milk. Bring the remaining milk to
the boil, stir a little of the boiling milk into the
cornflour mixture, then stir the cornflour mixture
into the simmering milk. Cook, stirring constantly,
until thick enough to coat the back of a spoon.

Remove from the heat, stir in the orange-flower
water and lemon zest, if used. Pour into a large
serving dish, or individual dishes and leave until a
skin forms on the surface. Sprinkle over the nuts.
Leave until cold, then cover and chill.

Sourdough Starter

*In the past, fresh yeast was scarce, or unavailable in North Africa, so a natural
sourdough starter was used for making breads. The mixture of flour and water is
activated by wild yeasts in the atmosphere and left to ferment before being
added to the bread dough. The starter can be kept alive for years – either just a
portion is used to make a loaf and the rest replenished with more flour and
water, or part of the bread dough is reserved to serve as the next batch of starter.*

115 g/4 oz plain flour
2 tbsp cornmeal (polenta)
1 tbsp groundnut oil

115–175 ml/4–6 fl oz
 lukewarm water

Sift the flour and cornmeal (polenta) together into a
bowl. Stir in the oil and 115 ml/4 fl oz water to form
a smooth dough. Transfer to a work surface and
knead in 1–2 tbsp water. Knead for 10–15 minutes
until the dough is smooth, shiny and elastic.

Sprinkle the dough with a little flour and form
into a ball that can be held in the hands. Put it in a
lightly oiled bowl, cover and leave for 12–24 hours
until double in bulk. The starter is now ready to use.

Rice Pudding

ROZ BIL HALIB

Rice pudding is popular throughout North Africa so it's not surprising that the people there really do know how to make a good rice pud (no shades of the UK school-lunch version). Cooked very gently for a long time, the rice is coaxed into absorbing plenty of milk, which makes a very creamy pudding. Almonds are often added to give more flavour; traditionally, the nuts would be pounded into almond milk by hand, but these days can be ground in a blender with hot water, straining the result, then repeating the process. A quicker and easier way is just to add freshly ground almonds to the pudding, with extra milk, which will make it even creamier and more flavoursome, and with a different texture.

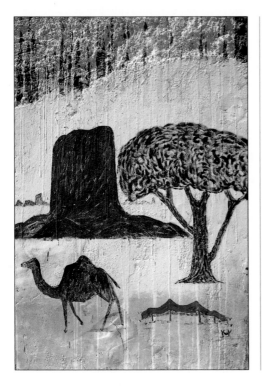

SERVES 4
approximately 1 ltr/1¾ pt
   milk
50 g/2 oz pudding (short-
   grain) rice, rinsed and
   drained

50 g/2 oz sugar
1–1½ tbsp orange-flower
   or rose water
chopped pistachio nuts or
   almonds, crystallized
   violets or roses

Heat the milk in a heavy, preferably non-stick, saucepan. Sprinkle over the rice and sugar and bring to the boil, stirring. Lower the heat then cook very gently stirring occasionally until the pudding is thick, velvety and falls easily from the spoon – this may take anything up to 2 hours; use a heat diffusing mat, if necessary, to prevent the rice cooking too quickly, and sticking. Stir in orange-flower water or rose water to taste. Pour into a serving dish, or individual dishes. Serve warm or cold with pistachio nuts, almonds, crystallized violets or rose petals scattered over.

LEFT *Wall painting near Tamanrasset, Algeria*

Moroccan Bread

KISRA/KHBOZ

Moroccan bread is round, golden and crisp-crusted. Country cooks often use all barley flour or cornmeal, or a mixture of two or three flours.

**MAKES 2 LOAVES, WITH
I LEFT TO USE AS A STARTER
(OR FERMENTATION ELEMENT)**

450 g/1 lb strong flour
4 tbsp cornmeal (polenta)
salt

*1 quantity Sourdough
    Starter (see page 108)
about 375 ml/13 fl oz
    warm water
sesame seeds or aniseed, if
    liked, for sprinkling*

Sift the flour, cornmeal and salt into a bowl. Add the Sourdough Starter then gradually mix in the water to make a smooth, pliable dough. Beat well then knead for 10–20 minutes until firm and elastic and the dough pulls away cleanly from the sides of the bowl.

Divide the dough into three; reserve one piece to use as a starter. With oiled hands, form the other two pieces into balls, sift a little flour over each then flatten to make 13 cm/5 in discs. Place on a floured baking sheet, cover and leave to rise until the dough springs back when pressed.

Preheat the oven to 200°C/400°F/gas 6. Prick each loaf three or four times with a fork, sprinkle with sesame seeds or aniseed if liked and bake for about 50 minutes until crisp and golden.

Light Buttery Biscuits

GHORIBA SABLE AU BEURRE

These Tunisian pastries show the French influence, both in name and in the use of butter. They can be flavoured with orange-flower or rose water.

MAKES ABOUT 30
375 g/13 oz plain flour
pinch of salt
225 g/8 oz icing sugar,
    plus extra for sprinkling

*135 g/4½ oz butter,
    chopped, melted and
    cooled*

Sift the flour and salt into a bowl and make a well in the centre. Slowly pour in the melted butter, gradually drawing in the dry ingredients to make a smooth dough. Shape into a ball, cover and chill.

Lightly butter two baking sheets. Knead the dough on a lightly floured surface until soft. Roll walnut-sized pieces into balls and press between your palms to flatten. Place well apart on the baking sheets. Chill for 20–30 minutes.

Preheat the oven to 180°C/350°F/gas 4. Bake the biscuits for 10–15 minutes until golden. Leave to cool on a wire rack then dust with icing sugar.

RIGHT *Moroccan Bread*

Raisin Doughnuts

———— SFENAJ ————

In Morocco the enticing smell of the doughnut-maker beckons people for their breakfast or a street snack. But making sfenaj *is not the prerogative of street doughnut-makers; they can easily be produced at home.*

SERVES 4–6

450 g/1 lb sugar

450 ml/³⁄4 pt plus 4 tbsp
  water

3 tbsp orange-flower water

225 g/8 oz strong white
  flour

2 tbsp lemon juice

pinch of salt

1¹⁄2 tsp easy blend yeast

25 g/1 oz raisins

1 egg

oil for deep frying

In a saucepan, gently heat the sugar and 450 ml/³⁄4 pt water, stirring until the sugar has dissolved. Raise the heat and boil until the syrup has reduced by one third. Remove from the heat and stir in the orange-flower water and lemon juice. Leave to cool.

Sieve the flour with salt into a mixing bowl, then stir in the yeast and raisins. Make a well in the centre.

In a jug lightly beat the egg with the remaining water then slowly pour into the well, drawing in the dry ingredients to make a smooth, soft dough, adding more water if necessary. Cover and leave until doubled in volume.

Turn the dough onto a floured surface and knead gently for 5 minutes. Divide the dough into 12 even pieces and roll each piece into a ball. Flatten the balls lightly and make a hole in the centre.

In a deep fryer or deep, sturdy saucepan, heat the oil to 180°C/350°F and fry a few doughnuts at a time for 5–8 minutes until golden. Using a slotted spoon transfer the doughnuts to paper towels to drain. Put them in a bowl, pour over the orange-flower water syrup and leave to soak for about 2 hours.

ABOVE *Dyeing vats in Fez, Medina, Morocco*

Almond Pastry Snake

M'HANNCHA

The Moroccan name for this rich, lightly perfumed pastry, means "the snake", accurately describing its coiled shape. M'hanncha will keep for several days if stored in an airtight container in a cool place, but not the refrigerator. Reheat gently before serving, if liked.

MAKES 12 PIECES
225 g/8 oz ground
   almonds
175 g/6 oz icing sugar
1 egg, separated
few drops of almond
   essence

1½ tbsp rose water
icing sugar for sprinkling
6 sheets filo pastry
4 tbsp melted butter or
   olive oil
icing sugar and ground
   cinnamon, to decorate

Stir the ground almonds and icing sugar together in a mixing bowl, then mix to a paste with the egg white, almond essence and rose water. Divide into 3 equal pieces. Sift icing sugar over the work surface then roll out each piece of almond paste to 48 cm/ 19 in long sausage, about 1.25 cm/½ in thick.

Brush a sheet of filo pastry with melted butter or oil then cover with a second sheet of pastry and brush that with butter or oil; cover the unused pastry with a damp cloth. Place one almond sausage along the length of the buttered or oiled pastry, about 2.5 cm/1 in from the edge. Roll up the pastry enclosing the almond sausage.

Form into a loose coil starting in the centre of a buttered or oiled 20 cm/8 in round loose-bottomed flan tin. Repeat with the remaining almond sausages and pastry. Join one to the end of the coil in the tin, and continue the coil outwards, then repeat with the last piece. Beat the egg yolk, in a small bowl, with a pinch of ground cinnamon, then brush over the top. Bake in a preheated oven 180°C/350°F/gas 4 for about 30 minutes until golden and crisp on top.

Remove the sides of the tin, carfully turn the coil over, replace on the bottom of the tin and return to the oven for a further 10 minutes, until the bottom is brown. Invert onto a cooling rack and leave to cool slightly. Sift over icing sugar then add lines of ground cinnamon to form a lattice pattern. Serve warm, cut into wedges.

Crisp Almond and Sesame Pastries

—————— SAMSA ——————

Like all Arab pastries, these from Tunisia are very sweet and only one or two can be eaten at a time. Fortunately, they do keep well when stored in an airtight container.

MAKES ABOUT 24
150 g/5 oz sugar
300 ml/¹/₂ pt water
1 tbsp lemon juice
orange-flower water
225 g/8 oz blanched
  almonds, lightly toasted
  and ground

1¹/₂ tsp finely grated
  orange zest
1¹/₂ tsp ground cinnamon,
  if liked
about 115 g/4 oz filo
  pastry
olive oil, for brushing
lightly toasted sesame
  seeds for sprinkling

Put the water and 115 g/4 oz of the sugar in a saucepan and heat gently, stirring until dissolved. Add the lemon juice and boil until syrupy. Remove from the heat and add the orange-flower water. Leave to cool.

Preheat the oven to 180°C/350°F/gas 4. In a mixing bowl, stir together the ground almonds, orange zest, cinnamon if using, and remaining sugar, then knead together the ingredients.

Brush one sheet of filo with olive oil; keep the other sheets covered with a damp cloth. Cut the oiled sheet into 3 lengthways strips. Place a small spoonful of filling at the bottom of each strip.

Fold the sides over the filling then roll the pastry up along the length. Brush inside the end of the pastry with oil and seal it to the roll. Brush with oil and put on a baking sheet. Repeat with the remaining pastry and filling. Bake the pastries for 15–20 minutes until crisp and golden.

Lower the pastries a few at a time into the hot syrup, leave for about 3 minutes so the syrup penetrates the pastries, then remove to a plate and sprinkle generously with sesame seeds. Leave until cold before serving.

ABOVE *Roman Amphitheatre, El Djem, Tunisia*

Pitta Bread

—————— PITA ——————

Although packets of ready-baked pitta bread are now available in North Africa,
some people still make their own dough and take it, ready-shaped to a baker, or
buy freshly baked bread from small shops, what are little more than kiosks in
the streets.
The dough can be flavoured with ground cumin or herbs, or brushed after
shaping with good olive oil and sprinkled with sesame seeds, or plenty of
"za'atar" mixed with salt.
To obtain the characteristic hollow, puffed shape, a very hot oven is needed
(traditionally this would be wood-fired), so be sure to turn the oven on well in
advance to give it plenty of time to heat up, but even then, some ovens may not
reach the necessary temperature. I also recommend preheating the baking trays
for 2 minutes. Alternatively, the breads can be cooked under a very hot grill.

MAKES ABOUT 12

15 g/½ oz fresh yeast or
1½ tsp easy-blend yeast
pinch of sugar, (if liked)
approximately 275 ml/
9 fl oz warm water

450 g/1 lb unbleached
strong white flour
salt
1 tbsp olive oil, plus extra
for brushing

Put the fresh yeast in a bowl, and if using with the sugar, blend in a little of the water then leave until frothy. Sieve the flour and a pinch of salt into a bowl. Stir in the easy-blend yeast, if using. Form a well in the centre. Pour the yeast liquid, if using, remaining water and the oil into the well and gradually draw the dry ingredients into the liquids, first using a wooden spoon then your hand. Mix to form firm, soft dough.

Turn the dough onto a lightly floured surface and knead for about 15 minutes until smooth and elastic. Generously oil a bowl, put the dough into it then turn the dough over to coat with oil. Cover and leave at room temperature until doubled in volume.

Turn the dough onto the work surface and knead briefly. Divide into 12 equal pieces. Flatten each piece with the palm of your hand to about 5 mm/ ¼ in thick and 10 cm/4 in in diameter. Brush with oil and place well apart on baking sheets. Cover with a lightly floured cloth and leave to rise for about 20 minutes. Preheat the oven to its highest setting.

Dampen the top of each piece of dough with cold water to prevent it browning. If cooking in the oven, using a fish slice, transfer some of the shapes to an oiled, preheated baking tray and bake for about 3 minutes, then lower the thermostat to 230°C/450°F/ gas 8 and bake for a further 2–3 minutes, until puffed and lightly speckled with brown.

If using the grill place the pieces of bread in turn under a very hot preheated grill, leaving them space to rise, and cook until puffed up and speckled with brown. Turn over immediately and leave for about 1 minute more.

Seal bread that is not to be eaten straight away in a plastic bag while still warm. For longer storage, freeze it, then reheat from frozen under the grill or in the oven. Bread that becomes dry can be refreshed by sprinkling with water then warming under a preheated grill or in the oven. To keep several loaves hot, wrap them in foil and put in the oven.

8

Spice Mixes, Sauces and Drinks

As alcohol is forbidden under Islam, other drinks replace wine. With such luscious fruits available, fruit juices and fruit-based drinks are popular. In Morocco sweet Mint Tea is *the* drink. Tea-making and drinking are taken very seriously and the whole process is surrounded by ritual and ceremony. Tea is drunk throughout the day, including at the end of a meal, anywhere, by any age group, for many contradictory reasons – as a restorative or sedative, as a medicine or a placebo.

Moroccan Spice Mix

——— RAS EL HANOUT ———

This recipe for fragrant spice mix (see page 11) has been simplified, which means it does, of course, lack some of the glory of a more complex blend.

MAKES ABOUT
2½ TABLESPOONS
6 allspice berries
4 cloves
1½ tsp black peppercorns

1¼ tsp coriander seeds
1 tsp cumin seeds
¼ tsp cayenne pepper
1½ tsp ground cinnamon
1 tsp ground ginger

Put all the whole spices in a grinder or pestle and mortar and work to a powder. Mix in the ground spices, then spoon into a glass bottle. Keep in a cool, dark place.

Za'atar

Za'atar can be mixed to a paste with olive oil and spread on bread before baking, used as a dip, and sprinkled on vegetables and meat balls. The blend can be stored for 3–4 months.

50 g/2 oz sesame seeds
25 g/1 oz powdered dried
   thyme

25 g/1 oz ground sumac

Heat the sesame seeds in a dry heavy frying pan, stirring frequently, until very lightly toasted. Allow to cool then mix with the thyme and sumac. Store in an airtight jar in a cool, dry, dark place.

Tunisian Five Spices

——— QALAT DAGGA ———

This blend is used in vegetable and lamb dishes. The spice called grains of paradise (Melegueta pepper) is a member of the cardamom family. The spice mix will keep for 3–4 months.

2 tsp cloves
2 tsp black peppercorns
1 tsp grains of paradise

1 tsp ground cinnamon
1 tsp freshly grated nutmeg

Grind the cloves, peppercorns and grains of paradise together in a grinder or pestle and mortar then mix with the other spices. Keep in an airtight jar in a cool, dry, dark place.

Tabil

Tabil *means coriander, but generally refers to this Tunisian spice blend, which includes coriander.*

2 tbsp coriander seeds
1 tbsp caraway seeds
4 garlic cloves

2 tsp crushed dried red chilli

Preheat the oven to its lowest setting. Pound all the ingredients together in a pestle and mortar, then spread over a baking tray and put in the oven for about 30 minutes until dry. Grind the dry ingredients to a fine powder. Keep in an airtight container for up to 4 months.

Harissa

Or "arhissa" as it is sometimes called, is a fiery paste based on chillies. It is primarily associated with Tunisia but it is also used in Algeria and Morocco. As well as being served as a condiment at the table, in a small dish with a small spoon, Harissa is used in cooking to add life to meat, poultry or vegetable casseroles, saffron-flavoured fish soups and stews, "stewed" red peppers and tomatoes. It is often used as a base for poached eggs, or added to dips, sauces and salad dressings.

50 g/2 oz dried red chillies, soaked in hot water for 1 hour
2 garlic cloves, chopped
2 tsp coriander seeds

2 tsp cumin seeds
2 tsp caraway seeds
pinch of salt
6 tbsp olive oil

Drain the chillies and put in a mortar, spice grinder or small blender with the garlic, spices and salt. Mix to a paste then stir in 3 tbsp of olive oil. Transfer to a small jar and pour a little oil over the surface. Cover and keep in a cool, dark place, or the refrigerator for 4–6 weeks.

Moroccan Butter

—— SMEN ——

This is a simplified way of making smen *(see page 11).*

450 g/1 lb unsalted butter, diced
1 tbsp coarse salt

¼ tsp herbes de Provence

Gently heat the butter in a saucepan until melted, then bring to the boil. Lower the heat and simmer for 3–4 minutes until the butter is clear and there is a separate layer on the bottom of the pan.

Line a sieve with muslin that has been wrung out in hot water, and sprinkle with the salt and herb. Gradually spoon the clear butter into the sieve and allow it to strain through. Then strain it again into a clean, dry jar. Cover and keep in the refrigerator for up to 6 weeks.

RIGHT *Harissa*

Almond Milk

—————— SHARBAT BIL LOOZ ——————

For the cleanest flavour, be sure to use fresh almonds.

SERVES 3–4
250 ml/⅓ pt cold milk
225 g/8 oz whole blanched
   almonds
225 ml/8 fl oz chilled
   water

caster sugar, to taste
rose water or orange-flower
   water, to taste

Mix the milk and almonds together in a blender until smooth. Strain through a sieve, pressing down hard on the sieve to extract as much liquid as possible.

Add the water to the almond milk then stir in sugar until it dissolves, and add rose water or orange-flower to taste. Chill before serving.

Apple Milkshake

—————— SARBAT ——————

A rich, cool drink made from milk and fruit or nut milk, sarbat *is an ideal "pick-me-up" for serving in the late afternoon on hot days when dinner will be late and something is needed to sustain guests through the early evening.*

SERVES 2–4
2 dessert apples such as
   Cox's Orange Pippin or
   Russet, peeled, cored and
   chopped

450 ml/¾ pt cold milk
2 tbsp caster sugar
about 1½ tsp rose water or
   orange-flower water
shaved ice, to serve, if liked

Put the apples, milk and sugar into a blender and mix until smooth. Add rose water or orange-flower water to taste. Serve over shaved ice, if liked, in chilled glasses.

Mint Tea

ETZAI

This light, sweet tea, particularly popular in Morocco, is made with green China tea and fresh spearmint. It is served as part of the traditional ritual of hospitality and the silver tea pot, sugar bowl and tray, the samovar and the ornately painted glasses and tea table can be quite magnificent.

1½ tbsp green tea
boiling water
3 tbsp sugar, or to taste

handful or fresh spearmint
  leaves

Put the tea in a 900 ml/1½ pt tea pot. Pour in a cupful of boiling water then immediately pour it out again; this is to wash the leaves. Add the sugar to taste, and the mint leaves. Pour in boiling water from a height of 30 cm/12 in (this oxygenates the made tea) and stir well. Serve the tea very hot, again pouring it from a height of about 30 cm/12 in.

LEFT *Apple Milkshake*

Lemons Preserved in Oil

This is an alternative way of preserving lemons, rather than packing them with salt (see opposite). The lemons are used to great effect with firm white fish (see Bream with Preserved Lemons, page 50). This recipe also works very well with limes.

4 large lemons
salt
few sprigs of coriander
2 plump garlic cloves,
    lightly crushed

1–2 dried red chillies
olive oil, to cover

Slice the lemons fairly thickly, discarding the pips. Sprinkle with plenty of salt and leave in a colander for 24 hours. Rinse and dry the lemons then pack into a clean, dry jar, inserting the coriander, garlic and chillies down the side of the jar as you go. Pour in olive oil to well cover the lemons. Swivel the jar to dispel any air bubbles. Cover the jar and leave for at least 1 month, swivelling the jar occasionally.

Preserved Lemons

Lemons lose their sharpness when preserved in salt and their unique flavour and silken texture is a characteristic of North African, and especially Moroccan, cooking. They also make a novel addition to non-Moroccan dishes. Preserved Lemons are easy to prepare; I have given two versions – one plain and the other with the less commonly used Safi spice mixture. Thin-skinned lemons will yield more juice. Once the jar has been opened the lemons will keep for up to a year, out of the refrigerator, but a layer of olive oil floated on the surface will help to preserve their freshness.

coarse salt

plump, juicy lemons,
preferably thin-skinned

Put 2 tsp coarse salt in a scalded Kilner or Parfait jar. Holding a lemon over a plate to catch the juice, and using a sharp, stainless-steel knife, cut lengthways as if about to halve the fruit, but do not cut quite through – leave the pieces joined. Ease out any pips. Pack 1 tbsp salt into the cuts, then close them and put in the jar. Repeat with more lemons, packing them tightly and pressing each layer down hard before adding the next layer, until the jar is full.

Squeeze the juice of another lemon over the fruit. Sprinkle with more coarse salt and top up with boiling water to cover the fruit. Close the jar tightly and keep in a warmish place for 3–4 weeks. Do not worry if, on longer storage, a lacy white film appears on top of the jar or on the lemons, this is quite harmless, and rinses off easily.

Note: If liked, a mixture of 1 stick of cinnamon, 3 cloves 6 crushed coriander seeds, 3 black peppercorns and 1 bay leaf can be layered with the lemons.

Chermoula 1

This is a recipe for a simple, basic all-purpose chermoula *that you can use as
a starting point to create your own versions for specific purposes. For example,
you can increase the amount of parsley, coriander, or chilli, add finely chopped
or grated onion, or adjust the ratio of the other spices.*

ENOUGH TO MARINATE A FISH
FOR 4 PEOPLE, OR MAKE A
SAUCE FOR 4
3 garlic cloves
salt
¼ dried red chilli, chopped
1½ tbsp paprika
1½ tbsp ground cumin

3 tbsp chopped fresh
   coriander
3 tbsp chopped fresh
   parsley
1 tbsp lemon juice
3½ tbsp white-wine
   vinegar
1½ tbsp fruity olive oil

Put the garlic, salt and chilli into a grinder and mix to
a paste. Mix in the ground spices and herbs then add
the lemon juice, vinegar and oil until smooth. Heat
gently in a saucepan until hot and fragrant, but do
not allow to boil. Leave to cool before using.

Chermoula 2

This is a more robust version of the chermoula *recipe above.*

ENOUGH TO MARINATE FISH,
POULTRY OR MEAT FOR
4 PEOPLE
1 Spanish onion finely
   chopped
2 plump garlic cloves,
   finely chopped
pinch saffron threads,
   lightly toasted and
   crushed

½ tsp ground cumin
¼ tsp paprika
pinch of cayenne
1 small bunch of mixed
   parsley and coriander,
   chopped
juice of ½ lemon
6 tbsp olive oil
salt

Mix all the ingredients together, as in the above
recipe.

Index